Therapeutics in Geriatric Neuropsychiatry

This publication was supported by an educational grant from

Wyeth-Ayerst Canada Inc.

Therapeutics in Geriatric Neuropsychiatry

Edited by

R.J. Ancill, S.G. Holliday and A.H. Mithani
Department of Psychiatry, St. Vincent's Hospital,
Vancounver, British Columbia, Canada

JOHN WILEY & SONS
Chichester · New York · Weinheim · Brisbane · Singapore · Toronto

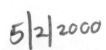
BAyshoRe

Other Wiley Editorial Offices

John Wiley & Sons, Inc., 605 Third Avenue,
New York, NY 10158-0012, USA

WILEY-VCH Verlag GmbH, Pappelallee 3,
D-69469 Weinheim, Germany

Jacaranda Wiley Ltd, 33 Park Road, Milton,
Queensland 4064, Australia

John Wiley & Sons (Canada) Ltd, 22 Worcester Road,
Rexdale, Ontario M9W 1L1, Canada

John Wiley & Sons (Asia) Pte Ltd, 2 Clementi Loop #02-01,
Jin Xing Distripark, Singapore 129809

Library of Congress Cataloging-in-Publication Data

Therapeutics in geriatric neuropsychiatry / edited by R.J. Ancill,
  S.G. Holliday & A.H. Mithani.
      p.   cm.
  Includes bibliographical references and index.
  ISBN 0-471-97947-3 (cased : alk. paper)
    1. Geriatric neuropsychiatry.   2. Aged—Diseases—Treatment.
  I. Ancill, R. J. (Raymond J.)   II. Holliday, Stephen, G.
  III. Mithani, A. H. (Akber H.)
    [DNLM: 1. Mental Disorders—in old age.   2. Geriatric Psychiatry.
  3. Neuropsychology—in old age.   WT 150 T398 1997]
  RC451.4.A5T46   1997
  618.97'689—dc21
  DNLM/DLC
  for Library of Congress   97–29971
                                                          CIP

British Library Cataloguing in Publication Data

A catalogue record for this book is available from the British Library

ISBN 0-471-97947-3

Produced from camera-ready copy supplied by the editors
Printed and bound in Great Britain by Bookcraft (Bath) Ltd, Midsomer Norton, Somerset
This book is printed on acid-free paper responsibly manufactured from sustainable forestation,
for which at least two trees are planted for each one used for paper production

5|2|2000

Contents

Contributors

Raymond J. Ancill, MB, FRCPC

Head, Department of Psychiatry, and
Director, Geriatric Psychiatry
Program, St. Vincent's Hospital
Vancouver, BC

Donald Calne, DM, FRCPC

Director, Neurodegenerative Disorders
Centre, Vancouver Hospital & Health
Sciences Centre, UBC Site
Vancouver, BC

Susan Calne, RN

Neurodegenerative Disorders Centre
Vancouver Hospital & Health
Sciences Centre, UBC Site
Vancouver, BC

Gergana Dimitrova, MD

University of Maryland Medical
Centre, Psychiatry Research Program
Baltimore, Maryland

Howard Feldman, MD, CM, FRCPC

Division of Neurology
University of British Columbia
Clinic for Alzheimer's Disease and
Related Disorders
Vancouver, BC

Marie Geizer, MD, FRCPC

Department of Psychiatry
St. Vincent's Hospital
Vancouver, BC

Cheryl Henry, MSW

Social Worker, Geriatric Psychiatry
Program, St. Vincent's Hospital
Vancouver, BC

Stephen G. Holliday, PhD, R.Psych

Director, Research & Education
Department of Psychiatry
St. Vincent's Hospital
Vancouver, BC

Stephen J. Kiraly, MD, FRCPC

Head, Endogenous Cortisol Research
Department of Psychiatry,
St. Vincent's Hospital
Vancouver, BC

Martin Illing, MD, FRCPC

Director, Inpatient Unit
Geriatric Psychiatry Program
St. Vincent's Hospital
Vancouver, BC

Lorraine Lyons, RPN, RN, BSN

Nurse Clinician
Department of Psychiatry
St. Vincent's Hospital
Vancouver, BC

Akber H. Mithani., MD

Medical Director, Geriatric Program &
Residential Care Program, CHARA
    Health Care Society
Director, Geriatric Education,
    Riverview Hospital
Clinical Associate Professor, The
    University of British Columbia

Lonn Myronuk, B.Sc (Psych), MD,
    FRCPC

Director, Postgraduate Education
Department of Psychiatry,
St. Vincent's Hospital
Vancouver, BC

L.James Sheldon, BSc (Pharm), MD,
    FRCPC

Director, Consultation/Liaison Service
Department of Psychiatry
St. Vincent's Hospital
Vancouver, BC

Catherine Schindell, RN, BSN

Nurse Manager, Department of
Psychiatry, St. Vincent's Hospital
Vancouver, BC

Paul Sungaila, PhD

Psychologist, Department of
    Psychiatry

Preface

Over the past twelve years, it has been my privilege to have had the opportunity to treat the elderly. Not only has this been challenging clinically, but it has been particularly rewarding. It was necessary for me to ensure that both my medical and psychiatric skills were up to the task and my diagnoses and therapeutic interventions were always scrutinized by colleagues and by students. This itself can be a sobering experience and one that geriatrics especially provides owing to the multidisciplinary team approach that care of the elderly requires.

The elderly patients themselves are rich in their history and experience. I have treated patients who were present at the Russian Revolution of 1917, who were at the Battle of Vimy Ridge in the First World War, who flew with Guy Gibson in the famous Dambuster raid in the Second World War, who survived Auschwitz and countless other witnesses to the history of the twentieth century. Unlike the Baby Boomers or Generation X, the elderly survived the Great Depression, fought for freedom against dictators and built the health care systems we all now enjoy. Yet at the very time they now need this health care system, it is often denied them. Fiscal restraint, no matter how well-intentioned, targets those that most need expensive inpatient and other services.

This has also been a decade of change in geriatric medicine and psychiatry. There has been a rapid growth in the geriatric subspecialties and both the Canadian Academy of Geriatric Psychiatry (CAGP) and the American Association of Geriatric Psychiatry (AAGP) are increasing their membership and take an active leadership role in training and establishing clinical standards.

Perhaps the most exciting phase lies just ahead of us. The first generation of antidementia drugs are appearing and their impact seems to be more than just increasing the MMSE by a few points. Those of us who have been fortunate enough to work with these compounds for several years have become impressed with the noncognitive improvements that can be achieved and several contributors to this book deal with this issue. Recognition is also given to the difficulty in obtaining data in this population in whom the traditional gold standard of "double-blind placebo-controlled" trials are both extremely hard to do and somewhat misleading even if ever achieved. Yet geriatric psychiatrists continue to strive to gather useful clinical data on newer, safer and effective treatments for a population characterized by complex presentations and intolerance of medications.

Therapeutics in Geriatric Neuropsychiatry is an attempt to bring to the reader an accumulation of clinical experience and is focused on the common clinical challenges of geriatric psychiatry. It is aimed at both specialists and general practitioners as well as nurses, psychologists and other health care professionals involved with this population. This book can be considered to have three distinct yet overlapping sections. One considers the neurodegenerative disorders both from a diagnosis and treatment point of view. Dr. Calne's chapter on Parkinson's disease is as thoughtful and informative as might be expected from one of the world's leading authorities in this area. Dr. Feldman writes succinctly about dementias of both vascular and Alzheimer's type drawing our attention to the novel treatments that are becoming available. Another section deals with the psychiatric syndromes and behavioural presentations from which elderly patients suffer whether they have a comorbid dementing process or not. Psychosis, depression, agitation and anxiety are covered in much detail as is the challenging syndrome of chronic pain. Dr. Myronuk and his colleagues tackle the place of electroconvulsive therapy in the elderly and this chapter is especially noteworthy for focusing on this necessary, safe and effective therapy. I am also pleased that we were able to incorporate a third section involving our colleagues in other disciplines — nursing, social work and psychology. The very nature of Geriatric Psychiatry is the multidisciplinary approach both to assessment as well as treatment. Finally, we have tried to draw attention to the problems inherent to research methodology in this population with the excellent chapter from Dr. Holliday and several of our colleagues. Probably nowhere in medical therapeutics is the incongruity between research populations and actual clinical practice so apparent as in geriatrics, yet research must continue and evolve if we are to move forward.

I hope that the reader will find *Therapeutics in Geriatric Neuropsychiatry* both stimulating and helpful. It is designed primarily as a clinician's handbook and represents the structure and framework of how we currently approach common neuromedical and psychiatric problems in the elderly. We realize there is yet much to learn and appreciate that we must always strive to do better. I trust and anticipate that practitioners in the future will correct the mistakes that we have made and that appear in this book.

Dr. Raymond J. Ancill
June 1997

1

TREATMENT OF PARKINSON'S DISEASE

Donald Calne and Susan Calne

Parkinson's disease (idiopathic Parkinsonism, (PD)) is a chronic, progressive, neurodegenerative disorder associated with loss of dopamine neurons in the substantia nigra. Several factors have been identified that cause a parkinsonian syndrome that is clinically similar to PD; these include neuroleptic use, manganese, viral infection and MPTP (Steck, 1954; Yamada, 1996; Calne et al., 1994a; Huang et al., 1993; Lin et al., 1995; Langston et al.; 1983).

The genetics of PD remain controversial but most researchers accept a major genetic contribution in about 15% - 20% of cases. Several studies have demonstrated low concordance in twins but, nevertheless, there exist large pedigrees of affected members (Ward et al., 1983; Wszolek et al., 1993; Wszolek et al., 1995). Recently, Polymeropoulous et al. have described an abnormality on chromosome 4q 21 in an Italian family with parkinsonism reported in detail by Golbe in 1993 and again in 1997 (Polymeropolous, et al., 1996; Golbe et al., 1993; Golbe et al., 1996). It is likely that research will ultimately demonstrate that there is more than one cause of PD with genetics determining susceptibility (Calne, 1994a; Calne, 1989; Huang et al., 1992).

PRESENTATION

Parkinson's disease is characterized by tremor, rigidity, bradykinesia and postural instability typically beginning on one side of the body. The diagnosis of PD may be problematic and a classification system exists defining criteria for

Therapeutics in Geriatric Neuropsychiatry. Edited by R.J. Ancill, S.G. Holliday and A.H. Mithani. © 1997 John Wiley & Sons Ltd

clinically possible, probable or definite PD (Calne et al., 1992). PD most commonly occurs over the age of 55 but 20% of patients seen in the Vancouver Hospital Movement Disorder Clinic develop the illness under the age of 50. Thirty percent of patients will not have tremor as a presenting feature, although it will usually emerge at some stage. As many as 50% of patients will experience an episode of depression during their illness and some 30% may develop features of dementia (Mayeux, 1987; Heitanen & Teräväinen, 1988). According to a careful study by Rajput et al. (1991), at least 35% of patients may be misdiagnosed in the first year of their illness. As a patient's illness evolves, a poor response to treatment and the development of atypical signs, may be indicative of the emergence of either multiple system atrophy, (MSA with profound autonomic failure), progressive supranuclear palsy (PSP with marked axial rigidity and paresis of vertical gaze), or prominent early dementia with parkinsonism (so called "Diffuse Lewy Body Disease").

PHARMACOLOGICAL TREATMENT

Treatment of PD is symptomatic and should begin when symptoms are having a significant impact on the patient's daily activities (Calne, 1993). A younger patient needing to work will probably start treatment sooner than a sedentary, retired person. In the geriatric population general principles of treatment must be tempered by the fact that when PD starts in older patients it progresses more quickly (Wolters et al., 1992). Elderly patients are more likely to be on medication for other medical conditions so they are at greater risk for complications and drug side effects (Calne et al., 1994b).

Levodopa used in conjunction with a decarboxylase inhibitor (Sinemet, levodopa/carbidopa; Prolopa[Madopar], levodopa/benserazide) is the most commonly used treatment. A controlled release preparation, Sinemet CR, provides a smoother, longer response than the standard release preparations. A normal starting dose of Sinemet CR is ½ a tablet a day, titrating to ½ a tablet 4 times a day over a period of 10-12 days. The most frequent early side effects are nausea and dizziness (caused by postural hypotension). These side-effects generally subside on their own, but if nausea requires immediate treatment it can be controlled with domperidone (an extracerebral D2 antagonist) 10 - 20 mg half an hour before each dose of levodopa preparation. If the addition of extra fluids and salt do not control hypotension fludrocortisone 0.1-0.2mg in the morning can be added. Midodrine 7.5 - 25mg daily is a useful addition to the fludrocortisone if required.

There is a commonly held misconception that levodopa preparations are only useful for a short period of time and that they should be withheld for as long as possible even in the face of symptoms that interfere with daily living. It has been established, however, that the problems associated with long term levodopa administration (wearing off, dyskinesias, and "on off" reactions) do not correlate well with either the length of time a patient has been on levodopa, or the amount of levodopa taken by the patient (Calne, 1994b; Calne, 1993; Huang et al., 1992; Rajput et al., 1991). Rajput and others have shown that timely administration of levodopa prolongs survival in Parkinson's disease (Diamond et al., 1987; Rajput et al., 1997). The misconception that levodopa is toxic in PD derives from experiments with high doses administered to cells in tissue culture-observations that have little relevance to the clinical situation.

With time and progression of symptoms, patients may develop "wearing off" reactions in which the prescribed dose of levodopa no longer controls their symptoms from dose to dose. Dyskinesia may also occur. When PD is in the advanced stage, unpredictable fluctuations in response to medications often develop. Of particular concern are "on off"- attacks, so called because of the speed with which they occur. Preventing and controlling "on off" attacks remains one of the greatest therapeutic challenges (Calne et al., 1994b).

When a patient is on 800 – 1000mg levodopa in Sinemet CR or 500-700mg standard Sinemet or Prolopa, and in need of more symptom relief, it is useful to add another dopaminomimetic drug typically bromocriptine or pergolide (Calne, 1994b).This, however, is not without risk as both are more frequently associated with such psychiatric side effects, such as hallucinations, than are levodopa preparations this point will be more fully explored in the section on changes in mental status. It is also important that a chest Xray be done prior to starting either bromocriptine or pergolide because of the rare, but reversible, complication of pulmonary fibrosis and pleural effusion (Bhatt et al., 1991)Another rare side effect is erythromyalgia with red, hot, painful feet and in the lower legs (Eisler et al., 1981).

The choice between bromocriptine and pergolide is a matter of physician comfort and experience, since the drugs have very similar actions (LeWitt et al., 1983). They do not cause dyskinesia when used by themselves de novo but they can exacerbate existing levodopa dyskinesia. However, they are not very effective when used on their own. However they can exacerbate existing levodopa induced dyskinesia. Levodopa can often be reduced when bromocriptine or pergolide is added. Bromocriptine 2.5mg, or pergolide .25mg are appropriate starting doses increasing to a stable dose over three - four weeks in outpatients (15 - 20 mg bromocriptine or 1.5 - 2mg pergolide). In hospital the doses can be increased more rapidly.

Anticholinergics and amantadine now play a small role in the management of PD as the side effects of confusion, and urinary retention tend to outweigh their therapeutic benefit. In addition, amantadine is excreted largely unmetabolised through the kidneys and should be used cautiously in patients with renal insufficiency. High tissue concentrations of amantadine or anticholinergics can cause psychosis. If these drugs have been taken for more than a month they should be withdrawn slowly over a period of 2-3 weeks (Calne, 1993).

Selegeline (deprenyl), a monoamine oxidase B inhibitor has a limited role in the treatment of PD. It can improve symptoms in early stages of the illness but its role as a neuroprotective agent is dubious and earlier claims must be re-evaluated in light of recent reanalysis of the data from the original DATATOP study (Schulzer et al., 1992). There have also been reports of atrial fibrillation, and increased mortality in patients taking this drug in combination with levodopa (Duarte et al., 1996; Lees, 1995).

SURGICAL TREATMENT

In the last 3-4 years pallidotomy has been revived as a treatment for PD (Laitinen, 1994). Pallidotomy was first performed in the late 1950's and its use eventually declined in favour of thalamotomy, which in turn declined following the development of levodopa. The recent resurgence in the use of pallidotomy has come about partly as a result of the availability of sophisticated imaging techniques (CT and MRI) which allow surgeons to place more precise lesions than were hitherto possible. Pallidotomy is known to improve rigidity and bradykinesia on the contralateral side; a serendipitous recent finding has been an observed, consistent, beneficial effect on levodopa induced dyskinesias. Dyskinesias are significantly improved on the contralateral side and, for unexplained reasons, some benefit occurs on the ipsilateral side as well. This observation has not yet been fully explained and may lead to a "re-drawing" of the anatomy of the brain and its pathways. Severe dyskinesia is a major indication for pallidotomy.

There is no upper age limit for this operation but patients should be in reasonably robust health (Kishore et al., 1997). Patients with dementia, or difficulty swallowing, should not undergo pallidotomy because these deficits may deteriorate following stereotactic procedures. In the University Hospital Movement Disorders Clinic it has been observed that patients who are depressed at the time of surgery may not be able to perceive any benefit following the operation and can pose a management problem. Depressed patients should be treated with an appropriate antidepressant prior to surgery.

Most centres are limiting pallidotomy to one side of the brain this reflects the current literature which indicates that bilateral pallidotomy significantly increases the risk of cognitive difficulties (Lozano et al. 1997). Deep Brain Stimulation is now being studied as a method of controlling symptoms on the unoperated side.

CHANGES IN MENTAL STATUS

As PD progresses, patients become more susceptible to medication side effects. In particular, therapeutic control of Parkinson symptoms can be complicated by a variety of changes in mental status. Treating clinicians should be sensitive to this situation as mental status changes are sometimes not easily observed and are often treatable.

Anxiety is a common occurrence and it is worth making sure that the anxiety is not coinciding with "off" periods, when an adjustment in antiparkinson therapy could help. Among patients attending the Movement Disorders Clinic at University Hospital, anxiety in combination with "off" periods is the main reason for Parkinson patients going to the emergency room. By the time the emergency room physician is able to see them they have often calmed down and their drugs are working appropriately. Patients and families need to be taught coping strategies to deal with anxiety. Severe bouts of anxiety constitute panic attacks, and lorazepam then becomes very helpful. When anxiety repeatedly threatens mobility patients can be taught to anticipate provocative circumstances and to take lorazepam ahead of time.

DEPRESSION

Depression occurs in up to 50% of patients with PD (Mayeux, 1987) and it may be present, often undiagnosed, before Parkinsonian symptoms appear. Sometimes depression will improve once treatment with antiparkinson drugs is initiated. However, physicians often have to make a judgement call as to which should be treated first, the depression or the Parkinsonism. Failure to deal with depression can lead to perceived failure of treatment for physical symptoms on the part of the patient, as well as an increase in psychosomatic complaints.

The diagnosis of depression is made clinically through interview and, if appropriate, through the use of rating scales. It is important to note that most standard rating scales such as the Hamilton Depression Rating Scale, include items measuring motor activity and that such items will be contaminated by the presence of Parkinsonian symptoms. The Beck Inventory of Depression is one instrument that does not rely on changes in motor performance and is a more effective screen for depression in PD (Beck & Beamesderfer, 1974). The Beck Inventory can be self administered at home and returned to the clinic by mail.

The most effective treatment for depression usually is antidepressant medication. Psychotherapy may be used as an adjunctive treatment, particularly if the person is having adjustment problems. It should be noted, however, that psychotherapy has not been shown to be effective with older patients. Younger patients may be more likely to benefit from psychotherapy if they are having difficulty adjusting to the diagnosis.

Venlafaxine and nortryptiline are the antidepressants of choice in our Movement Disorders Clinic. Venlafaxine has the double advantage of working quickly without lowering blood pressure. Hypotension can be a significant complication of antiparkinson therapy and tricyclic drugs will exacerbate this. Amytriptiline causes more hypotension than nortryptiline and doxepin is often too sedating. Nortryptiline is usually the best tolerated tricyclic antidepressant when given at suppertime in doses ranging from 25- 50 mg. In our experience serotonin reuptake inhibitors are often poorly tolerated in PD, causing nausea, an increase in tremor, and agitation.

In cases of intractable depression, electroconvulsive therapy (ECT) can be useful and it has the advantage of also improving Parkinsonian symptoms. Following treatment, patients can be maintained on a small maintenance dose of an antidepressant. Information on the benefits and safety of ECT should be disseminated more widely because, at present, many patients, often encouraged by their relatives, refuse ECT wrongly seeing it as a radical or dangerous treatment.

DEMENTIA

Neurologists debate whether dementia in PD is concurrent Alzheimer's disease or a Parkinson form of dementia. For the spouse or caregiver the debate is academic; they know the burden of care will increase regardless of etiology. It is important to rule out treatable causes of dementia and, in particular, the depressive pseuo-dementia sometimes seen in severely depressed patients. When a patient with PD presents with dementia, the patient must walk a tightrope trying to get as much mobility as possible from the antiparkinson drugs without making the dementia worse by inducing confusional side effects.

DRUG INDUCED MENTAL CHANGES

Parasomnias (nightmares and vivid dreams) can occur in the course of exposure to any dopaminomimetic preparation (Sinemet, Prolopa, bromocriptine or pergolide). Such dreams are sometimes described as very noisy and even physically violent. In some cases, the patient may end up on the floor and the spouse may feel the bed is a battlefield rather than a place of rest. This situation can sometimes be avoided, or ameliorated, by scheduling the last dose of drug(s) several hours before bedtime.

Any dopaminomimetic agent can cause mild hallucination. They can occur when the patient is responding well to medication and do not correlate to the age of the patient. In all other respects mental function can be normal. Mild hallucinations are seldom frightening to the patient, who usually recognises them as unreal. With bromocriptine and pergolide they frequently take the form of visions of small animals or children. The patient may chose to live with these hallucinations if the antparkinson drugs are providing an otherwise satisfactory level of mobility (Calne, 1993).

Psychotic and confusional states can also occur, with or without dementia. Treatable causes always need to be ruled out and the caregiver is often a vital source of information. The following questions can be helpful:

1. Have the drugs been taken properly over the last few days?
2. Has another drug been ordered?
3. Has the patient had a recent general anaesthetic?
4. Has the patient been given Demerol postoperatively?
5. Has the patient had a fever with or without a known infection?
6. Has the patient travelled recently through several time zones?
7. Is the patient constipated?
8. Has the weather been unusually hot and is the patient dehydrated?
9. Has the patient just been admitted to hospital?
10. Is the patient taking alternative health supplements?

When these possibilities have been ruled out, the antiparkinson drugs need to be considered because they can produce both psychosis and confusion. Both dose changes and withdrawals should be considered. Anticholinergic agents and amantadine should be reduced first and they may have to be stopped altogether. Bromocriptine and pergolide are the next group that should be withdrawn. Unfortunately, with dose reductions and withdrawals, the level of mobility is likely to deteriorate. If this happens there are options available. If there is no dementia, ECT is an effective treatment for dopaminomimetic psychosis and often the dose of antiparkinson drugs need not be reduced (Hurwitz et al., 1988). In addition ECT often improves Parkinsonian symptoms. Four to 6 treatments are usually sufficient. Patients are usually admitted to hospital for the first series of treatments but follow-up ECT can often be given as an out-patient.

If the patient is unsuitable for ECT because of concurrent dementia, frailty or prejudice, small doses of clozapine (Wolters et al., 1989) or the newer agent, olanzapine, are useful. The dose used is very much smaller than that employed for schizophrenia, 12.5 mg bid for clozapine or 2.5mg bid for olanzapine.

The use of conventional neuroleptics is seldom indicated. Giving conventional neuroleptics to patients with PD is functionally equivalent to reducing the dose of antiparkinson drugs while adding a sedative. Even some of the newer neuroleptics such as risperidone can lead to a worsening of parkinsonian symptoms. Clinicians should also be aware that sedated bradykinetic patients are at risk for potentially fatal pneumonia. Using conventional neuroloeptics, in short, may have a devastating effect on the PD patient.

SWALLOWING, MOBILITY, AND SAFETY

Patients with swallowing difficulties are at risk for choking, aspiration, and poor drug intake. Swallowing difficulties can be disproportionate to a patient's other symptoms. This is a major treatment consideration as there are no parenteral antiparkinson drugs available. Every attempt must be made to allow sufficient levodopa intake to maintain the integrity of the swallowing reflex. This will often mean a switch from a controlled release levodopa preparation to crushed regular levodopa and careful attention to determine whether the drug has been swallowed or has ended up coating the mouth, or is under the tongue. Patients cannot be left alone to take their drugs if their swallowing or mental status is impaired. Delivering drugs and nutrition via a gastrostomy feeding tube can improve a patient's mobility, safety and caloric intake.

Without adequate drug intake all mobility is restricted. The quality of life is reduced, and the patient is at risk for falls, aspiration pneumonia, urinary tract infections, and death. For patients with PD, even routine surgery on the gastrointestinal tract can require a nasogastric tube to ensure adequate drug delivery in the postoperative period. Failure to provide drug therapy renders the patient bradykinetic and at risk for pneumonia and emboli.

Rehabilitation Services should be consulted when patients need to make decisions about what assistive devices are needed. If the patient is reporting falls in the home it may be helpful to obtain an in-home OT/PT assessment. Often the home is a minefield of rugs, end tables, and tight corners. We should remember that a spouse's reluctance to change the status quo is often a last attempt to retain some control over the environment that is increasingly taken up with assistive devices and the needs of the patient.

If there is orthostatic hypotension, the caregiver can usefully monitor the lying and standing blood pressure, and the patient should be particularly cautious not to stand after exercise or after a hot bath/shower, or a meal.

How much exercise a patient can undertake will depend on the level of disability. As a general principle, attempts at ADL or exercise should be undertaken when drug efficacy is at its best. A safe, known environment best suits patients. In the poorly drug-controlled frail or confused patient, trips outside the home may generate great anxiety. This may, in turn, lead to a deterioration of all symptoms and the precipitation of an "off" reaction.

FINAL OUTCOME

It is now increasingly evident that PD "runs its course", and "burns itself out". This offers some support to the hypothesis that PD is the result of "an event" rather than a "process" (Calne, 1994a). Most, but not all patients live for years during which their illness is having a significant impact on their lives and of those close to them. We can observe this effect in patients with 'late stage illness' who return to the clinic year after year with no obvious sign of progression. The final years of a patient's life may be cruelly protracted and their medical management frustrating.

REFERENCES

Beck AT, and Beamesderfer A (1974) Assessment of depression: the depression inventory. *Modern Problems of Pharmacopsychiatry*, 7: 151-169

Bhatt M, Keenan SP, Fleetham JA and Calne DB (1991) Pleuropulmonary disease associated with dopamine agonist therapy, *Ann Neurol* 30: 613-616

Calne DB (1989) Is "Parkinson's disease" one disease", *J Neurol Neurosurg Psychiatry* 52: 18-21

Calne DB, Snow BJ, Lee C (1992) Criteria for diagnosing Parkinson's disease, *Ann Neuro,* 32 Suppl: S125-S127

Calne DB (1993) Treatment of Parkinson's Disease, *New England Journal of Medicin* 329: 1021-1027

Calne DB (1994a) Is idiopathic parkinsonism a consequence of an event or a process?, *Neurology* 44: 5-10

Calne DB (1994b) Early versus late combination therapy of dopamine precursors and dopamine receptor agonists, In: Wolters EC (ed*) Current Issues in Neurodegenerative Diseases, Volume 3. Parkinson's Disease: Symptomatic versus Preventive Therapy* (1994). ICG Publications, Dordrecht, pp 73-78

Calne DB, Chu N, Huang C, Lu C, and Olanow W (1994a) Manganism and idiopathic parkinsonism: Similarities and differences, *Neurology* 44:9: 1583-1586

Calne DB Duvoisin RC, Koller WC (1994b) Individualizing therapy in patients with disabling Parkinson's disease symptoms, *Neurology* 44 (Suppl 1): S8-S11

Diamond SG, Markham C, Hoehn M, McDowell FH, Muenter M (1987). Multi-Centre Study of Parkinson mortality with early versus later dopa treatment,*Ann Neurol* 22: 11

Duarte J, Alumina JV., Sevillano MD, Guerrero P, Barrero A, Claveria LE.(1996) Atrial fibrulation induced by selegeline, *Parkinsonism and Related Disorders* 2: 125-127

Eisler T, Hall RP, Kalavar KAR, Calne DB (1981) Erythromelalgia-like eruption in parkinsonian patients treated with bromocriptine, *Neurol* 31: 1368-1370

Golbe LI, Lazzaini AM, Schwarz KO, Mark MH, Dickson DW, and Duvoisin RC. (1993) Autosomal dominant parkinsonism with benign course and typical Lewy-body pathology, *Neurology* 43: 2222-2227

Golbe LI, Di Iorio G, Sanges G, Lazzarini A.M, La Sala S, Bonavita V, Duvoisin RC (1996) Clinical genetic analysis of Parkinson's disease in the Contursi kindred, *Annals of Neurology* 40: 767-775

Heitanen M, Teräväinen H (1988) The effect of age of disease onset on neuropsychological performance in Parkinson's disease, *J Neurology Neurosurgery and Psychiatry* 51: 244-249

Huang C-C, Lu C-S, Chu N-S, Hochberg R, Lilienfeld D, Calne DB (1992) Pathogenesis of idiopathic parkinsonism. In: Rinne UK, Yanagisawa N (eds) *Controversies in the treatment of Parkinson's disease*. PMSI, Tokyo, Japan, pp 7-13

Huang C-C, Lu C-S, Chu N-S, Hochberg R. Lilienfeld D. Olanow W. Calne DB (1993) Progression after chronic manganese exposure", *Neurology* 43: 1479-1483

Hurwitz T.A, Calne DB, Waterman K (1988) Treatment of dopaminomimetic psychosis in Parkinson's disease with electroconvulsive therapy, *Can J Neurol Sci* 15: 32-34

Kishore A, Turnbull IM, Snow BJ, De La Fuente-Fernandez R, Schulzer M, Mak E, Yardley S., and Calne D.B. (1997) Efficacy, stability and predictors of outcome of pallidotomy for Parkinson's disease. Six month follow-up with additional 1-year observations, *Brain* In press.

Laitinen LV (1994). Ventroposterolateral Pallidotomy,. *Stereotact Funct Neurosurg* 62: 41-52

Langston JW, Ballard PA, Tetrud JW, Irwin I (1983) Chronic Parkinsonism in humans due to a product of meperidine-analog synthesis, *Science* 219: 979-980

Lees AJ (1995) Comparison of therapeutic effects and mortality data of levodopa and levodopa combined with selegiline in patients with early, mild Parkinson's disease, *Br Med J* 311: 1602-1607

LeWitt PA, Ward CD, Larsen TA, Raphaelson MI, Newman RP, Foster N, Dambrosia JM, Calne DB (1983) Comparison of pergolide and bromocriptine therapy in parkinsonism. *Neurology* 33: 1009-1014

Lin SK, Lu CS, Vingerhoets FJG, Snow B, Schulzer M, Wai YY, Chu NS, and Calne DB (1995) Isolated involvement of Substantia Nigra in Acute Transient Parkinsonism: MRI and PET Observations, *Parkinsonism and Related Disorders* 1: 67-73

Lozano AM, Lang AE, Galvez-Jimenez N, Miyasaki J, Duff J, Hutchinson WD (1997) Effect of GPi pallidotomy on motor function in Parkinson's disease, *Lancet* 346: 1383-1387

Mayeux R (1987) Mental State. In: Koller WC (ed) *Handbook of Parkinson's Disease*. Dekker, New York, pp 127-144

Polymeropolous MH, Higgins J, Golbe LI, Johnson WG, Stenroos ES, Pho LT, Schaffer AA, Lazzarini AM, Nussbaum RL, Duvoisin R (1996) Mapping of a gene for Parkinson's disease to chromosome 4q21-q23, *Science* 274: 1197.

Rajput AH, Rozdilsky B, Rajput A. (1991). Accuracy of clinical diagnosis in Parkinsonism: A prospective study, *Can J Neurol Sci* 18: 275-278

Rajput AH, Utti RJ, Rajput A., Offord KP (1997) Timely Levodopa (LD) administration prolongs survival in Parkinson's disease. In: 12 edition. pp 121

Schulzer M, Mak E, Calne DB (1992) The antiparkinson efficacy of deprenyl derives from transient improvement that is likely to be symptomatic, *Ann Neurol* 32: 795-798

Steck H (1954) Le Syndrome extra-pyramidal et diencephalique au cours des traitements au Forgactil (chlorpromazine) au Serpasil (reserpine), *Ann Med Psychol* 1/2: 737-743

Ward CD, Duvoisin RC, Ince SE, Nutt JD, Eldridge R, Calne DB (1983) Parkinson's disease in 65 pairs of twins and in a set of quadruplets, *Neurol* 33: 815-824

Wolters EC, Hurwitz TA, Peppard RF, Calne DB (1989) An antipsychotic agent for Parkinson's disease, *J Clin Neuropharmacol* 12:2: 83-90.

Wolters EC, Tsui J, Calne DB (1992) Idiopathic Parkinsonism: More Rapid Progression in Late-Onset Patients. In: Hefti F, Weiner WJ (eds) *Progress in Parkinson's Disease Research*. Futura Publishing Co., Inc. Kisco, N.Y. pp 171-175

Wszolek ZK, Cordes M, Calne DB, Munter MD, Cordes I, Pfeifer RF (1993) Hereditary Parkinson's disease: report on three families with autosomal-dominant inheritance pattern, *Nervenarzt* 64: 331-335

Wszolek ZK, Uitti RJ, Calne DB (1995) German-Canadian family (family A) with parkinsonism and amotrophy-longitudinal observation. In: 242 edition. pp S71

Yamada T. (1996) Viral etiology of Parkinson's disease: focus on influenza A virus, *Parkinsonism and Related Disorders* 2: 113-123

2

TREATMENT OF VASCULAR COGNITIVE IMPAIRMENT/VASCULAR DEMENTIA

Howard Feldman

INTRODUCTION

The role of cerebrovascular pathology in the genesis of cognitive impairment and dementia has been increasingly recognized in recent years (Rockwood et al., 1994). It is now appreciated that a broad range of ischemic and hemmorhagic cerebrovascular injuries can produce both cognitive impairment and full blown dementia. An estimated 25% of patients presenting with stroke, at three months post event, are found to have dementia according to DSM criteria while there is a nine times increased risk of dementia following stroke (Tatemichi et al., 1992). A specific relationship between stroke and Alzheimer's disease (AD) has been recently elucidated whereby cerebrovascular lesions, insufficient to cause dementia on their own, have been shown to hasten both the onset and decline in Alzheimer's disease (Snowdon et al., 1997). A reported 15-30% of individuals with AD have neuropathological evidence of comorbid cerebrovascular injury (Gearing et al., 1995; Verhey et al., 1996). Accordingly, there emerges a wider array of potential treatment targets which will need to be investigated to provide optimal care to individuals that sustain cerebrovascular injury and who are at risk of vascular cognitive impairment (VCI), vascular dementia (VaD) and AD.

Novel therapeutic agents are emerging with potential applicability to many parts of the above disease spectrum. This chapter will review the conceptual basis of both vascular cognitive impairment and dementia, the mechanisms of cerebrovascular

Therapeutics in Geriatric Neuropsychiatry. Edited by R.J. Ancill, S.G. Holliday and A.H. Mithani. © 1997 John Wiley & Sons Ltd

injury and the treatment strategies, particularly pharmacological, that are emerging.

CONCEPTUAL BASIS OF VASCULAR DEMENTIA AND VASCULAR COGNITIVE IMPAIRMENT

DIAGNOSTIC ISSUES

The point at which vascular injury produces a definable dementia has eluded consensus and remains controversial. It has been clearly shown that the (Verhey et al., 1996) incidence of "vascular dementia" (VaD) will be determined by the diagnostic criteria that are applied. This has in turn lead to arguments that vascular dementia is either over diagnosed or under diagnosed (O'brien, 1988; Brust, 1988). It can be appreciated that DSM-IV criteria (APA, 1994) which anchor on impaired new learning and short term memory loss will overlook individuals as being demented who clearly have major cognitive and important behavioural changes with functional decline from cerebrovascular injury that happens not to involve temporolimbic structures. Erkinjuntti and Hachinski (1993) have argued that the focus should turn to a broader concept of vascular cognitive impairment (VCI) to describe the decline in a person's cognitive abilities, with concurrent changes in personality and mood that occur with cerebrovascular injury. The early recognition of VCI is emphasized with concern that by the time DSM-IV VaD criteria are met it will be too late to make effective intervention.

A number of sets of alternative VaD diagnostic criteria have been proposed during the last twenty years. Particularly in the past five years, there have been new diagnostic criteria sets proposed which integrate CT/MRI findings and which address the need for clinical radiological correlations. The State of California Alzheimer's Disease Diagnostic and Treatment Centres criteria (ADDTC) (Chui et al., 1992)and the NINDS-AIREN criteria (Roman et al., 1993) are currently the VaD diagnostic criteria of choice and the most frequently applied sets in clinical research studies. They differ however significantly in approach (Table 1) (Verhey et al., 1996; Amar et al., 1996). The NINDS-AIREN criteria utilize a traditional approach to defining dementia with specification that there should be memory impairment plus two other cognitive domains involved. The California criteria specify that there is a deterioration from prior known level of function which is not isolated to a single category of intellectual function. The NINDS-AIREN criteria include a broader range of cerebrovascular mechanisms than do the ADDTC criteria. The former criteria including hemmorhage and leukoariosis. Each of these disorders can be treated medically while their risk of causing VCI or VaD is uncertain.

TABLE 1: Summary of the main ADDTC and NINDS-AIREN criteria

	The ADDTC Criteria	The NINDS-AIREN Criteria
Dementia Definition	Deterioration from a known level of intellectual function sufficient to interfere with the patient's customary affairs of life, and which is not isolated to a single category of intellectual performance.	Impairment of memory plus at least two other areas of cognitive domains, which should be severe enough to interfere with activities of daily living and not due to physical effects of stroke alone.
Probable VaD	Requires all the following: 1. Dementia 2. Evidence of two or more strokes by history, neurological signs, and/or neuroimaging, or a single stroke with a clear temporal relationship to the onset of dementia. 3. Evidence of at least one infarct outside the cerebellum by CT or T1-weighted MRI.	Requires all the following: 1. Dementia 2. Cerebrovascular disease: focal signs on examination + evidence of relevant CVD by brain imaging (CT/MRI). 3. A relationship between the above two disorders, manifested by one or more of the following: (a) dementia onset within 3 months of a stroke (b) abrupt deterioration in cognitive functions, or fluctuating stepwise course.
Possible VaD	1. Dementia and one or more of the following: 2(a). History or evidence of a single stroke without a clear temporal relationship to dementia onset or 2(b). Binswanger's disease that includes all the following: (i) early onset of urinary incontinence or gait disturbance; (ii) vascular risk factors; (iii) extensive white matter changes on neuroimaging.	May be made in the presence of dementia and focal neurological signs in patients with: 1. No evidence of CVD on neuroimaging; or 2. In the absence of clear temporal relationship between stroke and dementia; or 3. In patients with subtle onset and variable course of cognitive deficit and evidence of CVD

Reprinted from K Amar, GK Wilcock, M Scott. The Diagnosis of Vascular Dementia in the Light of the New Criteria. Age Ageing 1996;25:51-55, by permission of Oxford University Press.

SUMMARY OF THE MAIN ADDTC AND NINDS-AIREN CRITERIA

Which of these or other criteria will be the most sensitive and specific criteria for VaD or VCI and which will become the gold standard is not presently clear. This represents a very critical research issue, particularly as it has been well demonstrated that these criteria are not interchangeable (Verhey et al., 1996).

NEUROPATHOLOGICAL AND NEUROIMAGING ISSUES

One of the early concepts of vascular dementia was that a volume of > 50 cc infarcted tissue could be associated with dementia while >100 cc would nearly always be associated with dementia (Tomlinson et al., 1970). It was the cumulative volume of infarction coupled to the presence of multiple, large and small thromboembolic cerebrovascular infarctions that became known as multiple infarction dementia (MID) (Hachinski et al., 1974). MID was estimated in most clinical pathological series of the era to account for 10-20% of dementia cases (Tomlinson et al., 1970), though Hachinski anticipated that MID would likely be over diagnosed due to coexistence with AD (Hachinski et al., 1974). It was noted that individual infarcts, insufficient to cause clinical events, could nonetheless in combination also lead to dementia (Hachinski et al., 1974).

With the advent of neuroimaging it has become clear that the volume of territory infarcted is only one mechanism by which vascular cognitive impairment or dementia can be produced. An additional mechanism is strategic infarction where ischemic lesions as small as 10 cc strategically located can contribute to or cause dementia (del Ser et al., 1990; Skoog et al., 1993). A list of such strategic infarctions capable of producing dementia is provided in Table 2.

Table 2. Areas of strategic infarcts producing cognitive impairment

•.Angular gyrus
•.Basal forebrain lesions
•.Non dominant parietal lobe
•.Thalamus including bilateral intralaminar nuclei
•.Posterior cerebral artery
•.Anterior cerebral artery

AREAS OF STRATEGIC INFARCTS PRODUCING COGNITIVE IMPAIRMENT

Neuroimaging has additionally enhanced the appreciation of smaller vessel vasculopathies both bilateral lacunar infarcts and subacute arteriosclerotic encephalopathy (Binswangers disease) that can act as a mechanisms of VCI and VaD. There continues to be debate as to the nature and effects of periventricular white matter changes which cannot be understood to invariably represent vascular infarction. There are a range of abnormalities that are identified in the periventricular white matter that range from perivascular edema to multiple small infarcts.[19] Hemmorhagic lesions from congophilic angiopathy, hypertensive hemmorhage, and aneurysmal subarachnoid bleeding can also produce VCI/VaD. Thus, it has become clear that there are a wide variety of mechanisms of vascular injury capable of producing VCI and VAD as outlined in Table 3.

Table 3. Proposed Causes of Vascular Cognitive Impairment

• Multiple cortical and subcortical infarcts (MID)
• Congophilic angiopathy
• Subacute arteriosclerotic encephalopathy (Binswanger's disease)
• Granular cortical atrophy (cortical microinfarction)
• Anoxic hypoxic encephalopathy
• Etat lacunaire
• Subacute diencephalic angioencephalopathy

PROPOSED CAUSES OF VASCULAR COGNITIVE IMPAIRMENT

In addition to these diagnostic considerations there is the unresolved issue of dual pathology or mixed dementia to consider. It has been well recognized that mixed or dual cerebral pathologies are not well separated by the Hachinski score which was devised to diagnose MID (Rosen et al., 1980). The potentially critical role of vascular injury in the pathogenesis of AD was emphasized by the recent study of Snowdon et (1997) where it was demonstrated that cerebrovascular lesions insufficient to cause dementia on their own can hasten both the onset and decline in Alzheimer's disease. The emerging awareness of both the accelerating effects of cerebrovascular disease on AD, as well as the presence of dual pathology, has renewed interest in pharmacological approaches which combine VaD and AD targets. However, there are presently no operational criteria to guide dual diagnosis.

TREATMENT STRATEGIES

PRIMARY PREVENTIVE MEASURES

Risk Factors: To date, there have not been any long term primary prevention trials for either VCI or VaD. The fundamental approach to primary prevention is likely to be based around the reasonable but unproven assumption that risk factors for VCI and VaD are the same as those for stroke (Evans, 1988). From the model of stroke, those risk factors which can be modified include hypertension, cardioembolic disease, diabetes mellitus, hypercholesterolemia, myocardial infarction and carotid artery disease. Lifestyle issues such as smoking, lack of exercise, diet and alcohol have been associated with cerebrovascular disease/stroke and could additionally be amenable to successful interventions if the assumption that stroke risk factors are of the same importance to the development of VCI and VaD.

Hypertension: Arguing for the treatment of hypertension as a preventive strategy are the observations that elevated systolic or diastolic blood pressure is independently associated with increased stroke risk irrespective of age (Wolf et al., 1992; Ott et al., 1995). There was a threefold increase in age adjusted risk of stroke for blood pressures above 160/95 mmHg in the Framingham study including the elderly sample (Wolf et al., 1992), while even modest increases in systolic blood pressure between 140-160 mmHg have been associated with increased stroke risk (Teal and Norris, 1997). The available data does not support the adage that acceptable or normal systolic blood pressure equals patient's age in years plus 100 mmHg (Teal and Norris, 1997). As the risk of stroke dementia from stroke increases significantly every 5 years from age 60 (Takemichi et al., 1992; Ott et al., 1995), a more aggressive treatment approach of hypertension needs to be considered as a strategy to prevent VCI and VaD.

Diabetes Mellitus: In diabetic patients there is a higher risk of cognitive impairment both in those who have sustained stroke as well as those who can be demonstrated to be at high risk of stroke (Takemichi et al., 1993). Both insulin dependent and non insulin dependent diabetics seem to be at higher risk of developing both vascular dementia as well as AD (Ott et al., 1996) Despite this well recognized risk, tight glycemic control has yet to be proven to reduce the risk of either initial or recurrent stroke and it remains to be shown that it can favourably influence the incidence of VCI and VaD (Teal and Norris, 1997). There is good evidence that favourable glycemic control will however lessen other diabetic complications including neuropathy.

Cardioembolic Stroke: Atrial fibrillation (AF), both chronic and paroxysmal, has been associated with increased stroke and dementia risk. The risk of dementia in association with AF increases with age (Ott et al., 1997), even when there is no history of stroke. There is a stratification of risk that can be constructed for AF. Nonvalvular AF carries a roughly fivefold increased stroke risk and estimated 4-5% annual increased risk while rheumatic mitral valvular AF has a much higher increased risk (Wolf et al., 1978). Atrial fibrillation in the Rotterdam study was also shown to have a stronger association with AD with cerebrovascular disease than with "pure" VaD. This supports the rational basis for treating atrial fibrillation to prevent the development of AD in at risk individuals (Ott et al., 1997).

Other cardiac sources of embolism include acute myocardial infarction, endocarditis and a dysfunctional left ventricle with thrombus. The aorta has been recognized to act as a further potential embolic source particularly during coronary bypass surgery, with increased embolic risk to aortic atheroma of >4 mm (Barbot et al., 1994). Each of these disorders has medical therapy though their risk of causing VCI or VaD is uncertain.

Asymptomatic Carotid Stenosis: Asymptomatic carotid stenosis carries a small increased annual risk of stroke of 1-2% (Norris et al., 1991; Anon., 1995b), while the risk of VCI or VaD remains ill defined. From the perspective of primary stroke prevention, despite the large trials with such acronyms as CASANOVA, ACAS and VA, it is still not resolved whether there are sufficient benefits to recommend endarterectomy or medical therapy as a stroke prevention for asymptomatic disease (Anon., 1991B, 1995a; Hobson et al., 1993). The current assessed benefits of surgery over medical treatment are currently considered to be marginal.

Lifestyle Risk Factors: Smoking has been reported to carry an increased odds ratio of 2 - 3.7 for stroke with a clear relationship to the number of cigarettes smoked (Colditz et al., 1988; Robbins et al., 1994). This risk extends across a variety of cerebrovascular mechanisms including ischemic cerebral infarction, subarachnoid hemmorhage and intracerebral hemmorhage. By contrast recent studies have not linked smoking to the development of VCI or VaD (Lindsay et al., 1997). The relationship of lipids to VCI and VaD is uncertain though serum cholesterol has been reported to be an independent risk factor for stroke (Iso et al., 1989). Alcohol, in light to moderate amounts, seems to be protective while larger amounts daily or in binges will actually increase ischemic and hemmorhagic stroke risk (Stampfer et al., 1988; Camargo, 1989). In the Canadian Study of Health and Aging (CSHA), alcohol abuse was identified as being a significant risk factor for vascular dementia (Lindsay et al., 1997).

The older studies of estrogen risk have been updated with recognition that there is no statistically significant increased risk of stroke with low dose oral contraceptives in premenopausal women (Lidegaard, 1993; Thorogood et al., 1992). There is some data to support a risk relationship being determined by the dose of estrogen. That is, there is an increasing odds ratio with increasing estrogen doses in a dose response relationship (Belchetz, 1994). Post menopausally the use of estrogens may actually be protective against both VaD and AD (Iso et al., 1989). Additional data will be needed to determine if estrogen use is associated with a relative risk reduction of VCI and VaD.

It is important to recognize that the known risk factors for stroke detailed above are additive, though their interactions in relationship to the development of VCI and VaD requires further research.

Primary preventive pharmacology: Antiplatelets and Anticoagulants

Antiplatelets: Aspirin has not been demonstrated to be beneficial in a number of studies undertaken for the primary prevention of stroke. There appears actually to be a slight increased risk of hemmorhagic stroke in individuals treated with ASA in patients considered to be at low risk. In a study with asymptomatic carotid stenosis of > 50% there were no significant differences in long term stroke rates (Cote et al., 1995) In the CSHA, current use of aspirin was associated with an odds ratio of 3.10 for VaD.

Anticoagulants: Warfarin has been demonstrated to be an effective treatment for primary prevention of stroke in patients with non valvular atrial fibrillation (Anon., 1994b). There is a less clear benefit risk ratio for those patients above the age of 75, who are at the greatest risk of VCI and VaD (Skoog et al., 1993). This appears to be due to the increased hemmorhagic complications of anticoagulation. In the elderly, risk stratification should be considered to aid the decision of anticoagulation of atrial fibrillation. Aspirin is an acceptable alternative for older patients with contraindications to warfarin (Anon., 1994c, 1996).

SECONDARY PREVENTION OF VCI AND VAD:

The risk of progressive VCI and VaD following an initial stroke has been variably estimated with confounders of varied demographics. Tatemichi et al. (1992) estimated that there is an odds ratio of 9.4 of dementia after stroke over the age of 60. It has also been demonstrated that dementia after stroke increases the risk of long term stroke recurrence, emphasizing the need for treatment of stroke risk factors (Moroney et al., 1997). Whether interventions following an initial vascular infarction influence the development of vascular cognitive impairment is not presently known and treatment options begin with those that have been studied for secondary stroke prevention.

Secondary Preventive Pharmacology: Antiplatelets and Anticoagulants

Antiplatelets: Though aspirin is widely used for the secondary prevention of stroke, individual studies comparing ASA with placebo show barely statistically significant benefit (Teal and Norris, 1997), whereas meta-analysis of pooled results has reported reduced fatal and non-fatal stroke rates as well as other vascular events including myocardial infarction (Anon., 1994a). The optimal aspirin dosage is controversial with inclusive evidence that 650-1300 mg/day (high dose) is better than 325 mg/day (intermediate dose) or 30-80 mg day (low dose) (Dyken et al., 1992). Whether there could be any benefit in relationship to periventricular white matter disease or no clinically apparent stroke has not been studied to date, nor is it clear that secondary prevention of clinical stroke will lessen the frequency of VCI and VaD. The current indications for aspirin as secondary prevention include the treatment of TIAs, minor strokes due to non-cardiac causes and those at risk for cardioembolic events who are unable and/or unwilling to take warfarin.

Ticlopidine has been shown to reduce risk of recurrent stroke, myocardial infarction, or vascular death by 23.3% compared to placebo in both men and women (Gent et al., 1989). In head to head trials with ASA for secondary stroke prevention following TIA and stroke, there has been statistically significant risk reduction for ticlopidine (Hass et al., 1989); however the enthusiasm for ticlopidine has been tempered by the 2.4% incidence of mild to serious bone marrow depression (Hass et al., 1989). This side effect is largely reversible if blood counts are monitored at two week intervals during the first fourteen weeks of therapy and if the medication is discontinued when WBC or platelet counts fall by more than 30%. There has not been adequate study of ticlopidine in relationship to cardioembolic stroke to recommend its use presently, though as with prevention of recurrent stroke it is indicated for those who are intolerant of ASA or who have had recurrent stroke on ASA. Whether ticlopidine has any efficacy in the secondary prevention of VCI or VaD is not determined at this time.

Anticoagulants: Warfarin has been demonstrated to be highly effective at reducing the risk of recurrent stroke in patients who have recently experienced TIA or stroke in the setting of non-valvular atrial fibrillation (relative risk reduction 69%) (Anon., 1994b). Anticoagulation with warfarin is significantly more effective than ASA with relative risk reduction of 62%. However, over the age of 75 the risk benefit ratio narrows and cardioembolic risk stratification is required with additional considerations of the mental status of the patient, gait stability, and likely compliance to the necessary procedures of anticoagulation.

Endarterectomy: From the NASCET study (North American Symptomatic Carotid Endarterectomy Trial), severe symptomatic carotid stenosis (ie>70%) with either transient ischemic attacks or small stroke carries a two year stroke risk of 26% for best medical management compared to 9% for carotid endarterectomy (Anon., 1991a). Thus, as a stroke prevention there is clear evidence for endarterectomy for the management of symptomatic carotid stenosis of > 70%. Symptomatic carotid stenosis < 70% has not yet been reported on by NASCET and best management is not yet settled. The incidence of VCI and VaD in this context is not presently known nor is the effectiveness of endarterectomy in secondary prevention.

SYMPTOMATIC AND STABILIZATION THERAPY FOR VCI AND VAD

There is no licensed drug in North America at this time for the specific treatment of either VCI,VaD, or mixed dementia. As in AD, it seems most reasonable to consider that interventions will produce either a symptomatic benefit of either short term (lines a+b) or longer term (lines a+c) or alternatively a disease stabilizing effect (line d) (Figure 1).

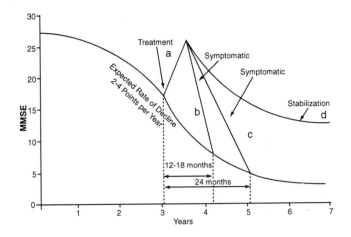

Figure 1. Hypothetical Projected Treatment Responses

For outcomes, a claim for symptomatic improvement will likely be made when there is cognitive enhancement and/or functional improvement over an appropriate time interval such as 6-12 months. Given the interrelationships of AD and stroke, it is likely that either or both cholinergic enhancing strategies and secondary stroke preventive measures will be investigated to demonstrate a symptomatic benefit on VCI and VaD.

When there is a longer term symptomatic effect over 12 months the question of whether the course of vascular dementia has been beneficially altered arises (i.e. stabilization effect). Different study designs will be needed to demonstrate that the divergence of treatment from placebo is sustained without crossover back to the placebo course. It is likely, that to produce such a stabilization effect on vascular dementia, there will need to be a significant effect on the underlying pathogenesis.

SYMPTOMATIC COGNITIVE ENHANCERS

Cholinergic Enhancement: It has been demonstrated in numerous randomized, double blind, placebo controlled studies that a variety of acetylcholinesterase (AchE) inhibitors can symptomatically improve cognitive function in Alzheimer disease patients (Knapp et al., 1994; Farlow et al., 1992; Rogers and Friedhoff, 1996; Anand and Gharabawi, 1996; Sramek et al., 1996). These therapies target the demonstrated cholinergic deficit in AD that has been well demonstrated in numerous studies (Whitehouse et al., 1986, 1988a,b) With the 30% incidence of dual pathologies in individuals with AD and vascular lesions, or as in NINCDS-ADRDA "possible Alzheimer's disease" where the possibility has been assigned on the basis of vascular injury, it is postulated that there could be significant cognitive benefits for treatment of such mixed dementias. Such clinical trials are currently being planned. There is no basis from established studies at the present time to recommend the use of cholinergic enhancers for VCI and VaD, though it is likely that such use will occur "off label". This potentially very important indication for this class of medications requires additional clinical trial investigation.

Vasodilators/Nootropics: In a review of forty-seven published randomized placebo controlled studies Schneider and Olin (1994) reported that, overall, ergoloid mesylates (hydergine) were more effective than placebo though the clinical benefits were "very modest at best". There was a dose-response relation noted. This suggests that higher doses than those approved could be more efficacious, though this is not yet well defined.

LONG TERM SYMPTOMATIC/STABILIZATION PHARMACOLOGIC THERAPIES

Propentofylline (HWA 285) is a compound currently in development that has a variety of mechanisms of action that make it favourable as a putative AD/VaD therapy particularly for longer term symptomatic use. It has been reported to act to block adenosine transport as a weak adenosine A1 receptor antagonist (Rother et al., 1996), while inhibiting both cAMP and GMP phosphodiesterase (PDE) (Parkinson et al., 1994). The resultant increase in cAMP leads to vasodilation, and inhibition of platelet aggregation amongst its effects. Additionally, it seems to have some effect on the formation and function of reactive microglia which have been postulated to form oxygen free radicals propagating the pathogenic cascade of VaD (McRae et al., 1994). At the level of producing symptomatic cognitive improvement, HWA 285 has been shown to improve learning and memory in rat experimental basal forebrain lesions with chronic treatment (Fuji et al., 1993), as well as stimulating long term potentiation in guinea pig hippocampus (Yamada et al., 1994). In experimental models of global and focal ischemia it has a neuroprotective effect reducing ischemic neuronal injury when administered both pre and post ischemic lesion (Parkinson et al., 1994).

In phase II and III clinical trial, preliminary reports have indicated that there have been favourable effects on cognitive and global outcome measures including the Syndrome Kurz Test (SKT), global assessment measure including the Gottfries Breen Stein (GBS) as well as on ADL scales (Rother et al., 1996) in both AD and VaD. These findings raise the possibility that propentofylline could be an effective therapy for AD, VaD or mixed cases. Further study reports of this compound are awaited.

CONCLUSIONS

The last several years have seen an updating of the older concepts of multiple infarct dementia, and the forthcoming era will see many studies on VCI, VaD and mixed dementia completed. The need for uniform sets of diagnostic criteria to be applied to such studies is emphasized as the criteria are not interchangeable. The results of therapeutic trials will be interpretable only if such criteria as the NINDS-AIREN or ADDTC are adhered to. Further clinical pathological correlative studies will be ongoing to better define the significance of subacute arteriosclerotic encephalopathy (Binswanger's disease) and other leukoariosis.

From a treatment perspective, the framework for interventions will include primary prevention, secondary prevention, symptomatic treatments and stabilization strategies. The overlap of comorbid AD and vascular injury will undoubtedly lead to clinical trials and experience treating both disorders with AD and VaD approaches. Propentofylline (HWA 285) represents the first approach which can rationally bridge this overlap and may find an indication for treatment of both AD and VaD. Other therapeutic aims will continue to focus on primary and secondary prevention with emphasis on both cognition and function as the key outcomes. The place of cholinergic enhancement and its utility in clinical practice for mixed dementia will require additional study.

The era of treatable Alzheimer's disease and both vascular cognitive impairment/vascular dementia appears to be emerging. A range of therapeutic targets have been identified ranging from risk factor and lifestyle management to more specific pharmacological approaches.

Acknowledgements: The capable assistance in the preparation of this work by Ms. Agnes Sauter is gratefully acknowledged.

REFERENCES

Amar K, Wilcock GK, and Scott M. (1996) The diagnosis of vascular dementia in the light of the new criteria. *Age Ageing* 25:51-55

Anand R, Gharabawi M (1996) An overview of the development of SDZ ENA 713, a brain selective cholinesterase inhibitor. In: Becker R and Giacobini E, eds. *Alzheimer Disease: From Molecular Biology to Therapy*. Birkhauser, Boston, 239-243

Anonymous (1991) Carotid surgery versus medical therapy in asymptomatic carotid stenosis. The CASANOVA Study Group [see comments]. *Stroke* 22:1229-1235

Anonymous (1991a) Beneficial effect of carotid endarterectomy in symptomatic patients with high-grade carotid stenosis. North American Symptomatic Carotid Endarterectomy Trial Collaborators [see comments]. *N Engl J Med* 325:445-453

Anonymous (1994) Warfarin versus aspirin for prevention of thromboembolism in atrial fibrillation: Stroke Prevention in Atrial Fibrillation II Study [see comments]. *Lancet* 343:687-691

Anonymous (1994a) Collaborative overview of randomised trials of antiplatelet therapy--I: Prevention of death, myocardial infarction, and stroke by prolonged antiplatelet therapy in various categories of patients. Antiplatelet Trialists' Collaboration [see comments] [published erratum appears in *BMJ* 1994 Jun 11;308(6943):1540]. *BMJ* 308:81-106

Anonymous (1994b) Risk factors for stroke and efficacy of antithrombotic therapy in atrial fibrillation. Analysis of pooled data from five randomized controlled trials [published erratum appears in Arch Intern Med 1994 Oct 10;154(19):2254]. *Archives of Internal Medicine* 154:1449-1457

Anonymous (1995) Endarterectomy for asymptomatic carotid artery stenosis. Executive Committee for the Asymptomatic Carotid Atherosclerosis Study [see comments]. *JAMA* 273:1421-1428

Anonymous (1995b) Risk of stroke in the distribution of an asymptomatic carotid artery. The European Carotid Surgery Trialists Collaborative Group [see comments]. *Lancet* 345:209-212

Anonymous (1996) Adjusted-dose warfarin versus low-intensity, fixed-dose warfarin plus aspirin for high-risk patients with atrial fibrillation: Stroke Prevention in Atrial Fibrillation III randomised clinical trial [see comments]. *Lancet* 348:633-638

APA (American Psychiatric Association) (1994) *Diagnostic and statistical manual of mental disorders (DSM IV)*. 4th ed., American Psychiatric Association, Washington DC,

Barbut D, Hinton RB, Szatrowski TP, et al. (1994) Cerebral emboli detected during bypass surgery are associated with clamp removal. *Stroke* 25:2398-2402

Belchetz PE (1994) Hormonal treatment of postmenopausal women [see comments]. [Review] [167 refs]. *N Engl J Med* 330:1062-1071

Brust JC (1988) Vascular dementia is overdiagnosed. [Review] [76 refs]. *Arch Neurol* 45:799-801

Camargo CA, Jr. (1989) Moderate alcohol consumption and stroke. The epidemiologic evidence. [Review] [109 refs]. *Stroke* 20:1611-1626

Chui HC, Victoroff JI, Margolin D, et al. (1992) Criteria for the diagnosis of ischemic vascular dementia proposed by the State of California Alzheimer's Disease Diagnostic and Treatment Centers. *Neurology* :42:473-480

Colditz GA, Bonita R, Stampfer MJ, et al. (1988) Cigarette smoking and risk of stroke in middle-aged women. *N Engl J Med* 318:937-941

Cote R, Battista RN, Abrahamowicz M, et al. (1995) Lack of effect of aspirin in asymptomatic patients with carotid bruits and substantial carotid narrowing. The Asymptomatic Cervical Bruit Study Group [comment] [see comments]. *Ann Intern Med* 123:649-655

Coyle JT, Price DL and DeLong MR (1983) Alzheimer's Disease: A Disorder of Cortical Cholinergic Innervation. *Science* 219:1184-1189 del Ser T, Bermejo F, Portera A, et al. Vascular dementia. A clinicopathological study. J *Neurol Sci* 96:1-17

Dyken ML, Barnett HJ, Easton JD, et al. (1992) Low-dose aspirin and stroke. "It ain't necessarily so" [editorial] [see comments]. *Stroke* 23:1395-1399.
Erkinjuntti T, Hachinski VC (1993)) Rethinking Vascular Dementia. *Cerebrovasc Dis* 3:3-23

Evans JG (1988) The epidemiology of dementias in the elderly. In: Brody JA and Maddox GL, eds. *Epidemiology and Aging: An International Perspective.* Springer, New York, 36-53

Farlow M, Gracon SI, Hershey LA, et al. (1992) A controlled trial of tacrine in Alzheimer's disease. The Tacrine Study Group [see comments]. *JAMA* 268:2523-2529

Fuji K, Hiramatsu M, Kameyama T, et al. (1993) Effects of repeated administration of propentofylline on memory impairment produced by basal forebrain lesion in rats. *Eur J Pharm* 236:411-417

Gearing M, Mirra SS, Hedreen JC, et al. (1995) The Consortium to Establish a Registry for Alzheimer's Disease (CERAD) Part X. Neuropathology confirmation of the clinical diagnosis of Alzheimer's disease. Neurology 45:461-466

Gent M, Blakely JA, Easton JD, et al. (1989) The Canadian American Ticlopidine Study (CATS) in thromboembolic stroke [see comments]. Lancet 1:1215-1220

Hachinski VC, Lassen NA, Marshal J (1974) Multi-infarct dementia: A cause of mental deterioration in the elderly. *Lancet* ;2:207-210

Hass WK, Easton JD, Adams HP,Jr., et al. (1989) A randomized trial comparing ticlopidine hydrochloride with aspirin for the prevention of stroke in high-risk patients. Ticlopidine Aspirin Stroke Study Group [see comments]. *N Engl J Med* 321:501-507

Hobson RW, Weiss DG, Fields WS, et al. (1993) Efficacy of carotid endarterectomy for asymptomatic carotid stenosis. The Veterans Affairs Cooperative Study Group [see comments]. *N Engl J Med* 328:221-227

Iso H, Jacobs DR, Jr., Wentworth D, et al. (1989) Serum cholesterol levels and six-year mortality from stroke in 350,977 men screened for the multiple risk factor intervention trial [see comments]. *N Engl J Med* 320:904-910

Knapp MJ, Knopman DS, Solomon PR, et al. (1994) A 30-week randomized controlled trial of high-dose tacrine in patients with Alzheimer's disease. The Tacrine Study Group [see comments]. *JAMA* 271:985-991

Lidegaard O (1993) Oral contraception and risk of a cerebral thromboembolic attack: results of a case-control study. *BMJ* 306:956-963

Lindsay J, Hebert R and Rockwood K. The Canadian Study of Health and Aging: risk factors for vascular dementia. *Stroke* 1997;28:526-530

McRae A, Rudolphi KA and Schubert P. (1994) Propentosylline depresses amyloid and Alzheimer's CSF microglial antigens after ischaemia. *Neuroreport* 5:1193-1196

Moroney JT, Bagiella E, Tatemichi TK, et al. (1997) Dementia after stroke increases the risk of long term stroke recurrence. *Neurology* 48:1317-1325

Munoz DG. (1991) The pathological basis of multi-infarct dementia. [Review]. *Alzheimer Dis Assoc Disord* 5:77-90

Norris JW, Zhu CZ, Bornstein NM, et al. (1991) Vascular risks of asymptomatic carotid stenosis. *Stroke* 22:1485-1490

O'Brien MD (1988) Vascular dementia is underdiagnosed. *Arch Neurol* 45:797-798.
Ott A, Breteler MM, de Bruyne MC, et al. (1996) Atrial fibrillation and dementia in a population-based study. The Rotterdam Study. *Stroke* 28:316-321

Ott A, Breteler MM, van Harskamp F, et al.(1995) Prevalence of Alzheimer's disease and vascular dementia: association with education. The Rotterdam study [see comments]. *BMJ* 310:970-973

Ott A, Stolk RP, Hofman A, et al. (1996) Association of diabetes mellitus and dementia: the Rotterdam Study. *Diabetologia* 39:1392-1397

Parkinson FE, Rudolphi KA and Fredholm BB (1994) Propentofylline: a nucleoside transport inhibitor with neuroprotective effects in cerebral ischemia. [Review] [43 refs]. *General Pharmacology* 25:1053-1058

Robbins AS, Manson JE, Lee IM, et al. (1994) Cigarette smoking and stroke in a cohort of U.S. male physicians. *Ann Intern Med* 120:458-462

Rockwood K, Parhad IM, Hachinski VC, et al. (1994) The diagnosis of vascular dementia: a consensus statement by the Consortium of Canadian Centres for Clinical Cognitive Research. *Can J Neurol Sci* 21:358-364

Rogers SL, Friedhoff LT (1996) The efficacy and safety of donepezil in patients with Alzheimer's disease: results of a US multicentre, randomized, double-blind, placebo-controlled trial. The Donepezil Study Group. *Dementia* 1996;7:293-303

Roman GC, Tatemichi TK, Erkinjuntti T, et al. Vascular dementia: diagnostic criteria for research studies. Report of the NINDS-AIREN International Workshop. Neurology 1993;43:250-260

Rosen WG, Terry RG, Fuld PA, et al. (1980) Pathological verification of ischemic score in differentiation of dementias. *Ann Neurol* 7:486-488

Rother M, Kittner B, Rudolphi K, et al. (1996) HWA 285 (propentofylline)--a new compound for the treatment of both vascular dementia and dementia of the Alzheimer type. [Review]. *Ann NY Acad Sci* 777:404-409

Schneider LS and Olin JT. (1994) Overview of clinical trials of hydergine in dementia [see comments]. *Arch Neurol* 51:787-798

Skoog I, Nilsson L, Palmertz B, et al. A population-based study of dementia in 85-year-olds. *N Engl J Med* 328:153-158

Snowdon DA, Greiner LH, Mortimer JA, et al. (1997) Brain infarction and the clinical expression of Alzheimer disease: The nun study. *JAMA* 277:813-817

Sramek JJ, Anand R, Wardle TS, et al. (1996) Safety/tolerability trial of SDZ ENA 713 in patients with probable Alzheimer's disease. *Life Sciences* 58:1201-1207

Stampfer MJ, Colditz GA, Willett WC, et al. (1988) A prospective study of moderate alcohol consumption and the risk of coronary disease and stroke in women. *N Engl J Med* 319:267-273

Tatemichi TK, Desmond DW, Mayeux R, et al. (1992) Dementia after stroke: baseline frequency, risks, and clinical features in a hospitalized cohort. *Neurology* 42:1185-1193

Tatemichi TK, Desmond DW, Paik M, et al. (1993) Clinical determinants of dementia related to stroke. *Ann Neurol* 33:568-575

Teal PA, Norris JW (1997) Modern stroke prevention. In: Batjer HH, ed.*Cerebrovascular Disease*. Lippincott-Raven, Philadelphia, 591-601

Thorogood M, Mann J, Murphy M, et al. (1992) Fatal stroke and use of oral contraceptives: findings from a case-control study. *Am J Epidemiol* 136:35-45

Tomlinson BE, Blessed G and Roth M. (1970) Observations on the brains of demented old people. *J Neurol Sci* 11:205-242

Verhey FRJ, Lodder J, Rozendaal N, et al. (1996) Comparison of seven sets of criteria used for the diagnosis of vascular dementia. *Neuroepidemiology* 15:166-172

Whitehouse PJ, Martino AM, Antuono PG, et al. (1986) Nicotinic acetylcholine binding sites in Alzheimer's disease. *Brain Res* ;371:146-151

Whitehouse PJ, Martino AM, Marcus KA, et al. (1988a) Reductions in acetylcholine and nicotine binding in several degenerative diseases. *Arch Neurol* 45:722-724

Whitehouse PJ, Martino AM, Wagster MV, et al. (1988b) Reductions in [3H]nicotinic acetylcholine binding in Alzheimer's disease and Parkinson's disease: an autoradiographic study. *Neurology* 38:720-723

Wolf PA, Cobb JL, D'Agostino RB (1992) Epidemiology of stroke. In: Barnett HJM, Mohr JP, Stein BM, et al, eds. *Stroke-Pathophysiology, Diagnosis, and Management.* Churchill Livingstone, New York, 3-27

Wolf PA, Dawber TR, Thomas HE, Jr., et al. (1978) Epidemiologic assessment of chronic atrial fibrillation and risk of stroke: the Framingham study. *Neurology* 28:973-977

Yamada Y, Nakamura H, Okada Y (1994) Propentofylline enhances the formation of long-term potentiation in guinea pig hippocampal slices. *Neurosci Lett* 176:189-192

3

PSYCHOSIS IN THE ELDERLY

Raymond J. Ancill

Psychosis in the elderly is common. Between 2% and 4% of the general elderly population has paranoid delusions and 13% of the mentally impaired elderly are either suspicious or paranoid (Lowenthal, 1964). However, whether these symptoms represent psychotic illnesses or are nonspecific presentations of neurodegenerative disorders is unclear but recent work suggests that cholinergic deficits, such as those found in dementia of the Alzheimer type, may present as psychiatric symptoms and may respond to cholinomimetic therapy (Cummings & Kaufer, 1996). Although Kraepelin coined the term "paraphrenia" in 1919 to describe patients who had paranoid delusions but lacked the emotional blunting of those with "dementia praecox" (Kraepelin, 1971), not until 1955 was it realized that for the majority of such patients, the onset of the illness was in the seventh decade of life (Roth, 1955). There is also controversy as to whether or not schizophrenia can emerge in late life, whether geriatric psychosis represents a quite distinct phenomenological entity, or whether paranoid delusions in the elderly are merely the manifestation of organic brain degeneration. These are not idle academic speculations. The use of neuroleptic medications in the elderly is widespread, even in those patients without psychosis, and these drugs are particularly toxic in this vulnerable population. A better understanding of the nature of psychotic symptoms in the elderly might, at the very least, identify those patients who might benefit from antipsychotic medications as well as those in whom such treatment would be better avoided and more appropriate therapies used.

Therapeutics in Geriatric Neuropsychiatry. Edited by R.J. Ancill, S.G. Holliday and A.H. Mithani. © 1997 John Wiley & Sons Ltd

Perhaps the commonest form of psychosis in old age is that associated with dementia, where it appears that there is a pervasive suspiciousness, which leads to memory being accounted for by paranoid or persecutory explanations. This is most evident when an elderly patient claims that a family member or residence manager is coming into their home at night and removing various items such as keys or groceries. The patient is unable to explain why this person is doing this or on what specific evidence they have concluded this. Clearly, the patient has forgotten where these articles were or has failed to purchase the groceries and is compensating for this memory difficulty with pervasive paranoid interpretations. Often there are accompanying auditory hallucinations of a "whispering" type. Unlike the hallucinations of schizophrenia or affective psychoses in younger adults, the auditory hallucinations in the elderly are rarely clear voices saying distinctive words or phrases. More often the elderly patient will state that they can hear people next door or upstairs or in the basement. The voices are muffled or whispering. It is likely that in this case, the patient has a persecutory interpretation of sensory noise due to impairment in hearing. Whether these are, in fact, hallucinations or a paranoid delusion is arguable.

However, the most contentious issue in geriatric psychosis is whether or not schizophrenia can emerge in late life. Certainly, the incidence of schizophrenia in the families of persons with an onset of paranoia in later life is increased (Funding, 1961; Rabins et al., 1984). But unlike classic schizophrenia which shows an equal sex incidence, late-onset psychosis demonstrates a preponderance of women (Kay and Roth, 1961; Marneros and Deister, 1984), this increased incidence in women as compared with men having been reported as high as II: I (Rabins et al., 1984).

Are there any other differences between early-onset schizophrenia (EOS) and late-onset "schizophrenia" (LOS)? Although cases of LOS demonstrate some familial clustering, the genetic contribution is weaker than has been found in EOS (Rabins et al., 1984). In LOS, there are significantly lower rates of formal thought disorder and the progressive deterioration in personality. This might imply perhaps that there are two distinct but overlapping populations with late-onset psychosis: the first is a form of late-onset schizophrenia but the second is consequent upon organic brain degeneration due to a variety of disorders. Certainly it has been shown that, as mentioned above, impaired hearing is associated with the development of psychotic symptoms in the elderly (Pearlson et al., 1989). It has recently been suggested that atrophy of the planum temporali is associated with the emergence of disordered thought and auditory hallucinations; this area is also involved in hearing and language comprehension. Thus injury to the planum temporali, whether early in life due to neurodevelopmental insults or later in life due to degeneration or ischemia, may alter the function of neuronal areas that involve hearing, language and thought (Rabins, 1994).

Whatever the etiology, the treatment of psychosis, whether in young adults or the elderly, does not depend on putative underlying causes. The use of antipsychotic medication is common in the elderly, even when psychotic features are absent, yet there are few studies indeed to support this widespread use. Furthermore, the elderly are particularly vulnerable to the side effects of these drugs which themselves can present with the apparent or superficial appearance of a psychosis.

Historically, phenothiazines (especially chlorpromazine and thioridazine) and haloperidol have been widely used in geriatric patients for behavioral control whether there was psychosis or not. The phenothiazines, although powerful tranquilizers, are particularly toxic, with such varied adverse events as postural hypotension, confusion, urinary retention, constipation, acute and tardive dyskinesias, blood dyscrasias, corneal opacities and jaundice. Haloperidol, being a potent but broad-spectrum dopamine blocker, does not have the same wide range of adverse events in the elderly but is very likely to produce disabling dyskinesias, both acute and tardive, even at low doses and even over periods as short as a few weeks. Certainly, when the patient is not even psychotic, potent nonselective dopamine-blocking agents such as haloperidol are best avoided, especially as haloperidol is not particularly tranquilizing. Loxapine is another neuroleptic that has been used quite widely, at least in Canada, for psychosis and for dysfunctional, aggressive behavior in the demented elderly. Although it is not an ideal drug, there is evidence to suggest it is significantly better tolerated than haloperidol in the elderly, especially in the area of extrapyramidal side-effects (Carlyle et al., 1993). More recently, risperidone has been introduced as a selective antipsychotic agent blocking D2 and 5-HT2 receptors. This has the net result of making risperidone a serotonergic antipsychotic by virtue of the fact that it blocks the postsynaptic serotonin "off-switch", thus allowing serotonin levels to rise while blocking D2 receptors selectively. There are, however, to date no published studies of the use of risperidone in the elderly.

A recent retrospective review of clinical experience of the use of risperidone in elderly patients with psychotic symptoms (Ancill & Nielsen, 1996) showed that even in patients intolerant of other neuroleptics, risperidone was both effective and well tolerated. Another naturalistic study comparing risperidone in young adults (mean age 41) and elderly patients (mean age 79) showed high compliance in both groups with good efficacy and a low-level of side effects. Of particular interest, this study demonstrated that the compliance rate was higher in the elderly group (80% versus 69.9% for adults) with a lower mean dose (1.26mg versus 4.37mg) and less side-effects (34.3% of elderly experienced mild side-effects as compared with 44.6% of the younger adults). It would, therefore, appear that risperidone is both effective and well tolerated in the elderly, which is a notoriously vulnerable population and that the doses required for efficacy are significantly lower than those required for adults. This may reflect a difference in pathologies accounting for the psychotic symptoms.

Newer antipsychotic agents such as the atypical neuroleptic, olanzepine, have yet to be fully evaluated for use in the elderly, but anecdotal evidence suggests that olanzepine is better tolerated in the elderly than is clozapine and there is currently no requirement for regular white blood cell counts with olanzepine. Olanzepine appears to be especially useful in elderly Parkinson's patients who require an antipsychotic for disease and/or drug related psychosis. Furthermore, many geriatric psychoses are resistant to typical neuroleptics and olanzepine may be an appropriate choice in these patients. In conclusion, psychotic phenomena are common in the elderly and even more so in the presence of a neurodegenerative illness. While there is controversy as to the underlying pathology of psychosis in the elderly, currently antipsychotic medications are the usual treatment. Traditional neuroleptics are especially toxic in the elderly but riperidone is much better tolerated and should be considered the first choice for the elderly. Olanzepine should be considered for special groups such as those with Parkinson's disease or who have failed a previous treatment.

REFERENCES

Carlyle W, Ancill RJ, and Sheldon LJ (1993) Aggression in the demented patient: a double-blind study of loxapine versus haloperidol. *International Clinical Psychopharmacology,* 103-108

Cummings JL, Kaufer, D (1996) Neuropsychiatric aspects of Alzheimer's disease: the cholinergic hypothesis revisited . *Neurology* 47, 876-883

Funding T (1961) Genetics of paranoid psychoses in later life. *Acta Psychiatrica Scandinavica,* 37:267-282

Kay DWK, Roth M (1961) Environmental and hereditary factors in the schizophrenia's of old age ("late paraphrenia') and their bearing on the general problem of causation in schizophrenia. *Journal of Mental Science* 107:649-686

Kiraly SJ, Gibson R, Ancill RJ and Holliday SG Risperidone: a comparative study of dosage, efficacy and side effects in adult and geriatric patients. *International Journal of Clinical Psychopharmacology,* in press

Kraepelin E. (1971)(original 1919). *Dementia Praecox and Paraphrenia,* translated by Barclay R.M. (eds Robertson GM., Huntington N.Y., and Kreiger R.E.)
Lowenthal MF (1964) *Lives in Distress,* New York, Basic Books

Marneros A and Deister A (1984) The psychopathology of "late schizophrenia". *Psychopathology,* 17:264-274

Peulson G, Kreger L, and Rabins PV (1989) A chart review of late-onset schizophrenia'. *AmericanJournal of Psychiatry,* 146:1568-1574

Robins PV (1994) Implications of late-life onset schizophrenia: a new hypothesis
In Schizophrenia: Exploring the Spectrum of Psychosis (eds Ancill R.J., Holliday S. and Higenbottam J.), John Wiley & Sons, Chichester.

Rabins PV, Pauker S, Thomas J (1984) Can schizophrenia begin after age 44?. *Comprehensive Psychiatry 25:290-293.*

Roth M (I 955) "The natural history of mental disorder in old age", *Journal of Mental Science, 101:281-301.*

4

DEPRESSION IN THE ELDERLY

Akber H. Mithani and Raymond J. Ancill

INTRODUCTION

Establishing a diagnosis of depression in an elderly patient can be both difficult and challenging. However, detecting and treating depressive syndromes in the elderly is immensely important as they have a tremendous impact on the elderly patient's functional abilities and quality of life. Estimates suggest that between 10 - 15% of elderly individuals living in the community have a clinically significant depression. The figure for facility populations is even higher with approximately 25 - 35% of residents in Residential Care Facilities suffering from a major depression.

It is very important to recognise depression in the elderly because:

1. Depression can greatly compromise the elderly person's functional abilities, often to the extent that they become unable to carry out activities of daily living and undergo a significant loss of independence.

2. Unrecognised depression, because of its affective and behavioural/functional consequences, can lead to increased caregiver stress.

3. The suicide rate for the elderly is two to three times higher than the rate for the general population. The elderly comprise of approximately 11% of the general population, however, 25% of suicides in the general population

Therapeutics in Geriatric Neuropsychiatry. Edited by R.J. Ancill, S.G. Holliday and A.H. Mithani. © 1997 John Wiley & Sons Ltd

occur in this age group. Suicide attempts by elderly people are much more likely to be successful than are attempts by people in other age groups. Elderly people, for example, have a much higher completion rate of suicide than do adolescents, a group recognised as having a high rate of suicide attempts.

4. Depression is highly treatable. Approximately 80% of major depressions can be successfully treated even in the presence of such dementing disorders as Alzheimer's disease and vascular dementia.

PRESENTATION

Many elderly patients do not present with the typical symptoms and signs of depression that are outlined in the standardised diagnostic schemes such as DSM IV and ICD X. Additionally, their depression is often complicated by multisystem organic diseases that may mimic, cause or exacerbate a mood disorder (see Figure 1).

S - Sleep

A - Appetite & Weight loss

M - Mood

T - Thought Disorder

E - Energy/fatigue & loss of interest

C - Cognition

Figure 1. Depression - Recognition

In our experience, the most commonly seen features of depression in the elderly are the   neurovegetative symptoms. The neurovegetative symptoms that characterize depression in the elderly are listed below.

a. Behavioural dysfunction such as psychomotor agitation
b. Diurnal variation in presentation, particularly if the presentation is worse in the morning.
c. Fitful sleep
d. Loss of appetite
e. Loss of weight

    f.   Psychotic features
    g.   Anergia and fatigue
    h.   Somatic complaints
    i.   Anhedonia

As noted above, suicide is a serious threat in the depressed elderly and every effort should be made to identify suicidal ideation or behaviour, including both active and passive (refusing food) categories of suicidal behaviour.

A minority of elderly patients will present with a more classic pattern of self-reported mood and affect changes and while the clinician should not overlook these symptoms, he should not over-emphasize them when establishing a diagnosis.

CAUSES

There are many factors that are associated with, and which may play precipitating or causal roles in, depression. These include:

    a.   *Predisposing Genetic Factors*. Depression and related disorders tend to run in families.
    b.   *Biochemical Factors*. Depression is known to be related to neurotransmitter imbalance in the central nervous system.
    c.   *Biological Conditions*. Parkinson's disease, Alzheimer's disease, cardiovascular disease and stroke can be associated with depression
    d.   *Psychosocial/environmental Events*. Significant events such as loss of a loved one, poverty, and loss of function due to medical illness may be precipitating, rather than causal, factors in the emergence of a depression. This is supported by the observation that although almost 100% of the elderly suffer such losses, only about 20% become depressed.

DIFFERENTIAL DIAGNOSIS

When establishing a diagnosis, it is important to consider the factors other than depression that can lead to the development of depressive symptoms. These include:

DISEASE

Many diseases may present as depression in the elderly. A partial list of the common disorders associated with depressive symptoms appears in Figure 2. At the minimum, a thorough medical history and a complete physical examination must be done to rule out these conditions.

- Malignancies - e.g. Pancreatic Ca
- Endocrine - e.g. Hypothyroidism, Cushing's
- Metabolic - e.g. Electrolyte imbalance, hypoxia, uremia
- Infection - e.g. Encephalitis, neurosyphilis, TB, AIDS
- Neurologic - e.g. Parkinson's, Huntington's
- Vitamin Deficiency - e.g. B12, niacin

Figure 2. Diseases that May Present as Depression in the Elderly

DRUGS

Elderly patients are likely to have multiple illness, and, consequently, they tend to be using multiple drugs. See Figure 3. Many of the drugs commonly used to treat physical illness may either cause or exacerbate depression. Therefore, care must be taken to elicit a detailed drug history and every reasonable effort should be made to reduce the intake of such drugs.

- NSAID's - e.g. Ibuprofen
- Antihypertensives - e.g. Propanolol, Methyl Dopa
- Hormones - e.g. Estrogen
- Alcohol
- Amphetamines
- H2 Blockers - e.g. Cimetidine
- Steroids
- Immunosupressants
- Benzodiazepines

Figure 3. Common Depressogenic Drugs

DEMENTIA

One of the more difficult clinical situations arises when the patient is demented and the question of a possible depression arises. From a historical perspective, the question has been whether it is possible to differentiate between dementia and depression ("depressive pseudodementia" in a cognitively impaired patient. While it is important to recognize that cognitive dysfunction may be a part of the clinical picture, more recent work has focused on the identification of the comorbid presentation of dementia and depression (Reifler, 1986; Ancill, 1993). Three lines of evidence support the notion that depression is a regular occurrence in the presence of dementia. First, in Alzheimer's disease there is a specific loss of norepinephrine neurones in the locus ceruleus. Second, patients with Alzheimer's disease are significantly more likely to have a previous history of late-life depression that predates the onset of the cognitive syndrome (Agbayewa, 1986). Third, Depression also occurs in a significant proportion of patients with other neurodegenerative diseases, such as Parkinson's Disease (Cummings, 1992). From a clinical viewpoint, it is important to note that response to treatment of depression is similar regardless of the presence or absence of a comorbid dementia (Ancill, 1989).

PHARMACOLOGICAL MANAGEMENT OF DEPRESSION

GENERAL PHARMACOLOGICAL ISSUES

The elderly have a more permeable, or "leaky", blood-brain barrier and therefore drugs will cross into the central nervous system much more readily than is the case with younger adults. This leaves the elderly patient at a higher risk of central nervous system side effects, including confusion, disorientation, hallucinations, delusions, dyskinesias and ataxia.

Significant changes in absorption, distribution, metabolism and elimination of drugs also occur as people age. From a clinical perspective, the elimination factor is the most important. Even when the blood urea nitrogen (BUN) and creatinine are within normal limits, the glomerular filtration rate (GFR) decreases exponentially with ageing. Drugs and their metabolites, therefore, tend to have a much longer half-life in the elderly and a substantially longer elimination time (calculated as five times the drugs, half-life) in elderly than in younger adults.

Compliance with medication regimes is also a major problem and it is estimated that fewer than 50% of adults are compliant to medications as prescribed. More disturbing is the fact that up to 70% of patients who discontinue their medications do so in the first seven days of therapy usually because of emergent side effects. The clinician can maximise the likelihood of compliance by spending enough time with the patient and their family to educate them about the medications.

TREATMENT OPTIONS

Various antidepressant classes are now available for the treatment of depression in the elderly. Of all the antidepressant classes available, the Specific Serotonin Reuptake Inhibitors (SSRIs), Reversible Inhibitors of Monoamine Oxidase (RIMAs) and the polytransmitter agents (SNRIs) have become the first antidepressant classes of choice for the treatment of depression in the elderly. Tricyclic Antidepressants, and other agents should only be used as second line treatment. Regardless of the class of drug, the patient must be on an adequate dosage of antidepressant for at least a minimum of *8 weeks* before achieving a complete response. The exception to this rule may be the SNRI venlafaxine with which efficacy may be achieved in a shorter period of time..

SEROTONIN REUPTAKE INHIBITORS

The specific serotonin reuptake inhibitors (SSRI) inhibit the reuptake of serotonin although it is unclear whether the antidepressant action is a result of this action. The SSRIs tend to have a more beneficial side-effect profile than tricyclic antidepressants, they are weakened anticholinergic agents and are unlikely to cause hypotension. Most are also not cardiotoxic and therefore much safer in overdose (Figure 4).

- **Advantages**
  - Effective with minimal toxicity
  - Mildly hypotensive
  - Non anticholinergic
  - Less sedating
  - Easy to administer
  - Well tolerated in elderly

- **Disadvantages**
  - Activating
  - Insomnia
  - GI side effects
  - ? less effective in psychotic depressions
  - Drug interactions e.g. with coumadin

Figure 4. Antidepressant Choices - SSRIs

Common side effects of SSRIs include gastrointestinal intolerance, headache, tremor, insomnia and agitation. In the case of patients with dementia, consideration must be given to the anti-cholinergic effects of the SSRIs and this must be weighed against the efficacy issue. Examples of serotonin reuptake inhibitors include:

1. Fluoxetine. This medication is nonhypotensive, noncardiotoxic and mildly anticholinergic. Side effects include nausea, nervousness, agitation (common in the elderly), insomnia, and diarrhoea. In the elderly, agitation is a common side effect. The initial starting dose in the elderly should be 2.5 to 5 mg per day, to be titrated upwards as tolerated. It is important to note that the major metabolite, norfluoxetine, has a very long half-life in the elderly population with elimination time of 60 to 90 days. Generally, this medication should not be used in geriatric patients.

2. Fluvoxamine. This medication is a serotonin reuptake inhibitor that is not hypotensive, noncardiotoxic and minimally anticholinergic. Side-effects include dizziness, nausea, nightmares and it is sedating. It is reasonably well tolerated in the elderly population and starting dose is 25 mg. Maintenance dose is in the range of 50 - 200 mg.

3. Sertraline. This agent is a more activating SSRI with side effects of diarrhoea, agitation, insomnia and nervousness. The starting dose of sertraline in geriatric patients is 25 mg given in the morning or at night depending on the effect of sleep. Maintenance doses range from 50 to 200 mg. In a recent case series carried out at St Vincent's Hospital Department of Psychiatry, many elderly patients intolerant of both tricyclics, such as nortriptyline, or the SSRI, fluoxetine, both tolerated and responded to sertraline at doses between 25 mg and 100 mg per day. Thus, setraline appears to be better tolerated in the elderly than is fluoxetine.

4. Paroxetine. Paroxetine is similar to the other serotonin reuptake inhibitors and has comparable efficacy. It is well tolerated in the elderly and has a short half-life of approximately one day and the advantage of having no active metabolites. It is anxiolytic and is useful to use in those patients who have a depression with features of anxiety or agitation. Clinically it is neither anticholinergic nor hypotensive although a small number of cases of inappropriate ADH secretion have been reported. The starting dose in the elderly is 5-10 mg. a day. 60% of elderly will respond to 20 mg per day as maintenance.

5.   Nefazodone. This medication is structurally related to trazadone and
     exhibits a "dual action" on the serotonin neurons. It is both a presynaptic
     SSRI and it is also an antagonist at the 5-HT2 receptors. By blocking
     serotonin reuptake, nefazodone increases the amount of serotonin in the
     synapse and by antagonizing the 5-HT2 receptors nefazodone helps
     facilitate increased neurotransmission at the 5-HT 1A receptor (it is thought
     that a decrease in 5-HT 1A receptor activity is important in the
     pathophysiology of depression). It is thought that nefazodone also helps to
     improve sleep quality by decreasing the time between the initiation of sleep
     and the first REM episode, increasing total REM sleep, and decreasing
     stage 2 sleep. It is minimally anticholinergic and there is some hypotension.
     There are also minimal cardiotoxic side effects. Major side effects include
     asthenia, dizziness, dry mouth, nausea and vomiting. The starting dose in
     the elderly is 50 mg at bedtime with maintenance being in the range 100-
     300mg also given as a night time dose.

In general, serotonin reuptake inhibitors are becoming popular for use in the
elderly population because of their side-effect profile. A general guideline for
the use of SSRIs is provided in Figure 5.

- Agitated Depression
    - Trazodone
    - Nefazodone

- Retarded/Anergic Depression
    - Sertraline
    - Fluoxetine (rarely)

- Nonspecific Depression
    - Paroxetine
    - Fluvoxamine

Figure 5. Use of SSRIs in the Elderly

REVERSIBLE INHIBITORS OF MONOAMINE OXIDASE

Reversible inhibitors of MAO (RIMA) such as moclobemide are well tolerated
in the elderly. Its mechanism of action is unique in that it increases
neurotransmitter availability by blocking enzymatic degradation. Also, its

inhibition of MAO-A enzyme is reversible which makes the old MAOI diet restrictions unnecessary for this agent. Side effects include insomnia, agitation, hypotension and nausea. The starting dose is 50 mg twice a day and elderly maintenance dose is about 600 mg a day. Post stroke depressions may respond particularly favourably to moclobemide. RIMAs, because of their lack of anticholinergic effect, may be useful in treating persons with co-morbid dementia and depression, especially as other RIMA compounds, such as lazabemide, are thought to be antioxidants and may be useful in certain dementias.

POLYTRANSMITTER AGENTS

An example of this newer class of antidepressants is venlafaxine. Venlafaxine inhibits the uptake of both serotonin and norepinephrine and, because of this dual action, has been termed an SNRI (serotonin-norepinephrine reuptake inhibitor). Venlafaxine also appears to be dopaminergic. It has been shown to be effective in the treatment of severe depressions and will often produce a response in patients who would otherwise go for ECT. Elderly dose ranges from 37.5 to 300 mg per day. Side effects include: asthenia, agitation, nausea, constipation, hypotension and hypertension. Although venlafaxine can be initiated at doses as small as 18.75 mg once or twice a day, most elderly patients will tolerate starting at a dose of 37.5mg BID. The commonest side-effect is nausea although in our experience it is no more likely than with the SSRIs. In any event, taking venlafaxine with food reduces the incidence of nausea even further.

Although venlafaxine is clearly indicated in more resistant and refractory depressions, it also has a role as a first line therapeutic agent, especially in those patients who have previously had a good effect from tricyclic antidepressants but can no longer tolerate the side effects. Patients with Parkinson's disease and depression and also patients who have not responded to an SSRI may also respond to venlafaxine. It may also prove to be an effective agent for person's with comorbid dementia and depression.

Therapeutic doses can be variable. Although many elderly patients will respond to 75 to 150 mg per day, doses of 300mg or even 450mg per day may be required.

TRICYCLIC ANTIDEPRESSANTS

There are two main types of tricyclic antidepressants - tertiary amines and the secondary amines.

The tertiary amines include amitriptyline, imipramine, doxepin, clomipramine and trimipramine. All of those compounds are strongly anticholinergic, hypotensive, antihistaminergic and cardiotoxic. See Figure 6. There is also a high incidence of delirium with the tricyclics. These compounds should NOT be used in the elderly population.

- Highly Anticholinergic
  - Vision problems leading to blindness
  - Constipation leading to obstruction
  - Delirium
  - Urinary retention
  - Severe dry mouth
- Highly hypotensive
  - leads to falls and fractures
- Cardiotoxic
- e.g. Imipramine, Amitriptyline

Figure 6. TCA - Tertiary Amines

The secondary amines are better tolerated in the general elderly population and if used correctly and sensibly, can be very effective. Examples are desipramine (which is the least anticholinergic) and nortriptyline (which is the least hypotensive). The secondary amines are still used in geriatric psychiatry (see Figure 7), where they are normally reserved for those patients requiring drug therapy who have not responded to the less toxic antidepressants. However, even the secondary amines carry significant risk to the frailer elderly and the emergence of the significantly safer venlafaxine has reduced our dependency on these compounds.

Advantages	**Disadvantages**
– Proven to be effective	– Antihistaminergic - quite sedative
– Compliance can be monitored with blood levels	– Cardiotoxic
– Cost	– Anticholinergic
– ? more effective in psychotic depressions	– Hypotensive
	– Lethal in overdose

Figure 7. Antidepressant Choices - Tricyclics

With the sole exception of lofepramine (only available in Europe), all tricyclic antidepressants are cardiotoxic and therefore full cardiac evaluation is essential before starting these medications as is regular monitoring during treatment.

OTHER ANTIDEPRESSANTS

Trazadone is a non-TCA compound with serotonergic, antihistaminic and mildly anticholinergic effects. Its side effects include sedation, hypotension and delirium. Priapism, although uncommon, has also been reported. The initial starting dose is 25 - 50 mg and usual maintenance dose is between l00 - 400 mg. The high maintenance dose required with trazadone increases the likelihood of side-effects in the elderly patient.

STRATEGIES FOR ACHIEVING MAXIMUM EFFICACY

There are many patients who have either a partial response or who fail to respond at all to the first prescribed antidepressant. For these patients, four drug management strategies can be applied: *optimization, substitution, combination and augmentation.*

Optimization. The goal of the optimization strategy is to ensure that the patient is treated with the *correct therapeutic dose* for an *adequate length of time.* In the elderly, the patient must be on an adequate dosage of antidepressant for a minimum of 8 weeks. The general rule of "start low, go slow" should be adhered to so that the patient can be maintained on a minimum effective dose.

Substitution. The substitution strategy involves substituting one type, or category, of drug for another. Although it can be an effective management technique, it is usually not a preferable option as it involves waiting an additional 8 weeks for the substituted agent to work. When practising substitution, the clinician should note that the SSRIs are reasonably different pharmacological compounds and can be substituted within the same class.

Combination. The combination strategy involves the use of combination of different classes of antidepressants. While there are no concrete rules, certain combinations may be specifically contraindicated. For instance, care must be taken when combining an SSRI with a TCA as the SSRIs can increase plasma levels of TCA.

Augmentation. The augmentation strategy is usually the best option for partial and nonresponders. There are many augmenting agents that are used (Figure 8), lithium being the most common. The addition of another agent may lead to compliance problems, which should be monitored closely.

- Lithium
- Triiodothyronine (T3)
- Buspirone
- Tryptophan
- Valproate
- Gabapentin

Figure 8. Augmentation Strategies

ELECTROCONVULSIVE THERAPY (ECT)

ECT is an extremely useful and important treatment modality for patients suffering from depression that is resistant to medications. It is also useful with patients who have medical contraindications to drug therapy. ECT is associated with a high efficacy and low morbidity and mortality. The indications in depression for the use of ECT are:

(a) The presence of life-threatening conditions, especially if the patient refuses to eat or drink or is suicidal
(b) The presence of depression that is resistant to pharmaco-therapy
(c) The presence of psychotic depression
(d) A history of responding to ECT.
(e) Patients who are medically fragile and likely to suffer serious medication side-effects.
(f) A request by the patient

There are no absolute contraindications to the use of ECT in the elderly. Relative contraindications are:

(a) Evidence of raised intracranial pressure
(b) Occurrence of a CVA (hemorrhagic) in the last 6 weeks
(c) Occurrence of a myocardial infarction in the last 3 weeks

(d) Presence of cerebral edema
(e) Presence of an unstable fracture

ECT is a safe procedure when administered properly and is an extremely effective one, which is probably under-utilised, in the geriatric population. There is no evidence that ECT cannot be safely and effectively used with patients who present with co-morbid dementia and depression. The available research (see Chapter 8 of this book) suggests that ECT neither impairs cognition, speeds up the course of dementia, nor otherwise negatively impacts on the dementia.

SUMMARY

Depression is difficult to diagnose in the elderly; treatment must be based on a biopsychosocial environmental model and drug therapy must be tailored to the individual's need and physical status. Drug management strategies and ECT are reasonable options in the elderly and follow-up of antidepressant therapy is absolutely essential.

REFERENCES:

Agbayewa MO (1986) Earlier psychiatric morbidity in patients with Alzheimer's disease. *Journal of the American Geriatrics Society* 34: 561-564

Ancill RJ (1993) Depression in Alzheimer's Disease: Confusing, confounding but treatable. In *The Management of Alzheimer's Disease*. (Ed. Wilcock GK), Wrightson Biomedical Publishing Ltd.

Ancill RJ (1992) Cognitive-affective disorders: the co-presentation of depression and dementia in the elderly. *Psychiatric Journal of the University of Ottawa*, 14, 370-371

Cummings J (1992) Depression and Parkinson's disease: a review. *American Journal of Psychiatry,* 149: 443-454

Katona CLE (1994). *Depression in old age",* West Sussex, England. John Wiley & Sons.

Martin L (1997) When an antidepressant fails. *Medicine North America*, 23-31.

Mithani A, Ancill RJ (1996) Helping your elderly patient cope with depression. *Medicine North America*, June: 27-36.

Reifler BV (1986) Mixed cognitive-affective disturbances in the elderly: a new classification. *Journal of Clinical Psychiatry* 47, 354-356

5

THE AGITATED AND AGGRESSIVE ELDERLY PERSON IN RESIDENTIAL CARE

Akber H. Mithani

INTRODUCTION

Agitation and aggression are extremely important management problems for those who deliver health care services to the elderly, both in hospitals and nursing homes. It is widely recognized that dysfunctional behaviour is often the final factor leading to loss of independent living and admission to long term or extended care facilities. Once admitted, the problems generally continue. Studies have shown, for example, that 48% of nursing home patients exhibit agitation and/or aggression. The problem is even more pronounced when residents are suffering from dementia and the available data suggests the prevalence rate for agitation and aggression can reach 85% in this group. Not only do aggression and agitation present significant management challenges, they impact on other services and patients. Admission of the elderly to psychiatric and medical units is often the result of behavioral disturbances, and the most common types are agitation and aggression. Examination of hospital admission data has also revealed that physical aggression is involved in approximately 10% of the fractures in the elderly. Given the extent of the problem and the potential for a serious negative outcome, it is critical that agitation and aggression in the elderly be accurately identified and effectively treated. The following material examines the diagnostic and treatment issues that are central to the management of agitation and aggression.

Therapeutics in Geriatric Neuropsychiatry. Edited by R.J. Ancill, S.G. Holliday and A.H. Mithani. © 1997 John Wiley & Sons Ltd

DEFINING AGITATION

Agitation is neither a diagnosis, syndrome, disease nor disorder. Rather, it is a symptom. Agitation is best thought of as a disturbance of psychomotor activity, which is characterized by increased motor activity, impulsive acts, vocalization, and behavior disturbances. Agitation has two major components: 1. A motor component and 2. A psychic component. Both components must be present to constitute agitation. The *motor component* is defined by increased motor activity. The motor activity may include aggressive acts or repetitive actions such as pacing. Pacing is a common form of agitation in the demented elderly. It differs from wandering both in its topography and in the fact that it often has an underlying medical cause. Agitated pacing is uncontrolled motor activity. Patients who pace seldom respond to redirection and often show accompanying signs of irritability, stress and anxiety. Elderly persons who pace can cover up to 20 km in a day, often in complete disregard of their physical state. This level of activity can lead to severely compromised cardiovascular and hemodynamic status and to increases in both morbidity and mortality. This contrasts with the behaviour of the person who wanders, and is typically responsive to re-direction as well as not being at risk for the above factors. Distinguishing between pacing and wandering is crucial as wandering seldom requires aggressive management while pacing typically requires both pharmacological and environmental interventions.

The *psychic component* of agitation is defined in terms of observable emotional distress in the individual. Without some indication of distress, the diagnosis of agitation must be questioned. Returning to pacing, as an example, people who pace often show marked distress. This distress can be expressed orally, either with words or sounds, or non-verbally through aggressive activity, facial expressions, and body-language such as writhing and twisting. Persons who wander, on the other hand, do not as a rule exhibit the same signs of distress and do not seem to be particularly disturbed by either the environment or their internal state.

IDENTIFICATION OF AGITATION

The assessment of agitation in residential care residents is challenging and is best done using an interdisciplinary approach. But regardless of the availability of a full interdisciplinary team, there are four key issues the examining clinician should carefully examine in order to determine the exact nature and cause(s) of the behavior.

THE TYPE OF BEHAVIOR

In gathering information on the behavior of the individual, the clinician should:

1. Document exactly what happened. Agitation is a term that typically means different things to different people. The onus is upon the clinician to concisely and comprehensively document the occurrence of a specific form of agitation.

2. Describe the actual events that occurred focusing on the antecedents of the behaviour, the reaction of staff and any other pertinent information, This information will be useful in determining the type of environmental interventions necessary to control the behavior.

3. Obtain accurate and complete collateral history from the spouse, caregiver or nurse. Since caregivers typically have a wealth of information about the resident, a careful interview can typically provide much useful information about both the genesis of the behaviour and potentially effective management approaches.

THE CHRONOLOGY OF THE BEHAVIOR

Documenting the temporal patterning of agitated behaviour is important and leads to information that is useful in establishing a diagnosis. For instance, if the agitation originates early in the day and improves as the day goes on, a diagnosis of depression may be considered. If the agitation originates later in the day it is suggestive of a diagnosis of anxiety. If the agitation takes place at night it is suggestive of a diagnosis of delirium. It is also very important to track the agitated behaviour against the backdrop of the person's daily routines. Many severely cognitively impaired elderly become agitated at certain times of high stimulation including change of shift, mealtimes, scheduled outings, and group recreational activities. In such cases, simple environmental manipulations may significantly reduce dysfunctional behavior.

THE PRECIPITATING FACTORS

It is important that the clinician consider the set of factors that are generally known to precipitate the agitation. If the agitation and aggression appears to be associated with external factors such as procedures of care (e.g., the timing of feeding, toileting or bathing, the approach to the person), then these factors can usually be controlled by environmental manipulation. The clinician also needs to rule out the possibility that underlying pain syndromes are being manifested as a behavior problem. (This point will be covered later in the chapter.) *Unprovoked* aggression, however, is usually the result of internal factors such as delirium or delusions, which may best be controlled through a combination of medications and environmental manipulation.

THE UNDERLYING DISEASES

Since, as I established earlier, aggression and agitation are symptoms, not diseases, it is essential to determine the underlying cause of these symptoms. It is only by doing so that it is possible to proceed with the effective management of agitation and aggression in the elderly. There are two main categories of underlying disease that are associated with agitation and aggression: systemic disorders and neuropsychiatric disorders. These categories are identified in Table 1.

Table 1. Common Causes of Acute Agitation in the Elderly

Elderly Systemic Disorder	Neuropsychiatric Disorders
Hypoxia e.g. CHF or COPD	Delirium
Hypo/hyper thyroidism	Agitated depression
Hepatic disease	Cognitive affective disorder
Renal failure	Normal pressure hydrocephalus
UTI (urinary tract infection)	CVA (cerebral accident)
Pneumonia	Subdural haematoma
Pain	Dyskinesia and Psychosis
Drugs	Drugs

The systemic disorders commonly associated with the emergence of agitation and aggression include hypoxia due to cardiac failure or chronic obstructive pulmonary disease, thyroid disorders, hepatic disease, renal failure, infections (e.g. urinary tract and respiratory infections), and, very importantly, pain. The neuropsychiatric disorders which commonly produce symptomatic agitation and aggression include delirium, agitated depression, cognitive affective disorder, normal pressure hydrocephalus, stroke, subdural haematoma, drug induced dyskinesia and psychosis (e.g. akathisia). It cannot be too strongly stressed that drug induced delirium is one of the most common causes of agitation and aggression in the elderly.

MANAGEMENT OF ACUTE AGITATION AND AGGRESSION

ACUTE PHARMACOLOGICAL MANAGEMENT

The most important principle in the management of acute agitation and aggression is treating the underlying cause. However, acute treatment of the agitation may be required in order to reduce the individual's discomfort and to control the dysfunctional behavior. The acute management of agitation in the elderly usually involves the administration of medications, typically neuroleptics and benzodiazepines.

Neuroleptics

Loxapine (Loxapac) is well tolerated in the elderly and is a good choice in the acute treatment of agitation and aggression. The dose ranges effective in this frail elderly population range from 2.5mg to 15 mg/d. Other neuroleptics, such as chlorpromazine and thioridazine (Thorazine), that are commonly used with younger populations are very hypotensive and anticholinergic, and are poorly tolerated by the elderly. However, methotrimeprazine (Nozinan) at a dose range of 2.5 to 10 mg/d is a good tranquilizer and reasonably well tolerated. Because of its sedating properties it is especially useful if the agitation is worse at night. Haloperidol (Haldol) is probably a poor choice since it is not a very effective tranquilizer and has comparatively higher extrapyramidal side effects that may actually worsen. Risperidone (Risperdal) at a dose range of 0.5 to 2.0 mg can be used effectively for the acute management of agitation. Unfortunately, risperidone is currently unavailable in intramuscular form. Zuclopenthixol acetate (Clopixol) at a dose range of 12.5 to 50 mg by IM injection is a good choice and a single IM dose can provide effective tranquilization for up to 48 hours.

Despite their proven effectiveness in short-term symptom management, neuroleptics must be used with caution in the elderly. The elderly, in general, and in particular elderly women and person suffering from dementia, are at significant risk for a number of serious side effects from neuroleptics. The risk factor for tardive dyskinesia is significantly higher and increases significantly with age and length of exposure to neuroleptics. Hence, it is imperative to wean the individual off the neuroleptics (following standard procedures) once the underlying disease has been identified and a proper long-term management plan initiated.

Benzodiazepines

Benzodiazepines may be indicated for individuals with agitation, particularly when the agitation is not accompanied by aggression. Commonly used benzodiazepines include lorazepam (Ativan) and alprazolam (Xanax). It is important to be extremely cautious when using these medications with the elderly, and to avoid the use of benzodiazepines with a long half-life. Lorazepam is the most widely used and the only benzodiazepine that is available in intramuscular form. It may, however, cause both cognitive deterioration and ataxia, the latter of which can result in falls and fractures. Alprazolam is both better tolerated in the elderly and less sedating, but may also cause ataxia. Benzodiazapines may also be useful as potentiating agents in patients who show a partial response to neuroleptics but who cannot tolerate higher doses of the medication.

PHARMACOLOGICAL MANAGEMENT OF CHRONIC AGGRESSION IN DEMENTIA

When patients present with dementia and with behavioral disturbance such as aggression there is inevitably a decline in the quality of life for both patients and caregivers. Even small improvements in these behaviors can result in a significant improvement in the quality of life of both patients and caregivers. In terms of the pharmacological management of chronic aggression in dementia, several types of medications may be useful including mood stabilizers, anitconvulsants, neuroleptics, beta-blockers, and antidepressants. Some of the more commonly used medications are reviewed below.

Carbamazepine (Tegretol): Carbamazepine has been shown to be efficacious in the treatment of chronic aggression with dementia. It is not currently used as a first line drug with the elderly as there are significant problems related to tolerability. Frequently observed side-effects include nausea, drowsiness, dry mouth, and ataxia. It may also cause bone marrow suppression and regular complete blood counts must be done to monitor for this side effect. Additionally, it has complex pharmaco-kinetic properties and, consequently, can be a difficult medication to manage in the elderly. Nevertheless, carbamazepine has been shown to be especially useful for patients who have abnormal EEGs with comorbid mood or personality disorders. Initial starting dose is about 200mg a day, up to 1800 mg a day.

Valproic Acid (Epival): Valproic acid exerts its CNS effect on the neurotransmitter GABA (gamma-aminobutyric acid). It has recently achieved some success in the treatment of chronic aggression in dementia and appears to both well-tolerated and effective. The starting dose is typically 125mg per day. Steady state dosages typically range from approximately 500 mg – 1250 mg. Although it is generally well tolerated, the more frequent side effects seen with this medication include nausea, vomiting, indigestion, weight gain, hair loss, tremor and increased appetite. Liver toxicity can also occur. Thrombocytopenia is a rare complication. Because of the possibility of serious side-effects, patients on valproic acid should be regularly and carefully monitored by the attending physician.

Gabapentin (Neurontin): This is a newer anticonvulsant and although it is chemically related to GABA, it does not appear to function through any previously recognized GABA receptor system. It has a very simple absorption and elimination pattern and has some properties of an amino acid. It does not break down in the liver and therefore has no effect on other drugs with hepatic metabolism. The drug is excreted through the kidneys and therefore the clearance of gabapentin is proportional to the creatinine clearance. It is very well tolerated in the elderly with starting doses of 100 to 200 mgm per day and steady-state dosages of 400 – 800mg per day.

Buspirone (Buspar): Originally introduced as an antipsychotic medication with some antidepressant properties, buspirone may be considered for treatment-resistant cases where the aggression has the associated features of anxiety or depression. Buspirone works very well as an anti-aggression drug in the elderly provided the dose is adequate. Starting dose is 5mg PO BID with increases up to 60 - 80 mg per day. Another significant feature of buspirone is its long half-life, and takes up to 8 weeks for full anti-aggressive effects to occur. Generally, Buspirone is very well tolerated with few side effects and is considered to be quite safe when used with the elderly.

Propranolol (Inderal): Propranolol can be used in the treatment of chronic aggression with dementia. The major limiting factor for the use of betablockers, though, is the side effects of hypotension and bradycardia and, therefore, these agents should be used with extreme caution. Because of these side effects, these drugs are not commonly used in the pharmacological management of aggression in the elderly.

Lithium: Lithium has long been successfully used in the treatment of chronic aggression in dementia. It should, however, be used with some caution in the elderly. Common side-effects of lithium include tremor, polydipsia and polyuria, flattening of T waves on EKG, GI irritability, disorientation, ataxia, hypothyroidism with goiter, aggravation of psoriasis, and sinus node dysfunctioning in the heart causing syncope. Pre-treatment evaluation for lithium is extremely important. The pre-treatment evaluation should include a full history, physical examination and a mental status examination. Lab investigations such as complete blood count, renal function tests, electrolytes, thyroid function tests, urinalysis and EKG should also be performed. The starting dose of lithium should be approximately 150mg per day and this should be titrated up to a level of 0.4 - 0.6mmol/L. Toxic levels occur beyond 0.8 or 0.9 mmol/L. The attending physician must be able to recognize the toxic side effects of lithium, especially nausea, vomiting, diarrhea, at which point lithium should be stopped as lithium toxicity can lead to seizures, delirium and even death.

Trazodone (Deseryl): Trazodone is an atypcal antidepressant that can be used quite effectively in the treatment of an agitated depression with aggressive components. The initial starting dose is 25 - 50 mg, with the maintenance dose being about 200 - 400 mg. Side effects include sedation, hypotension and delirium.

AGGRESSION AND THE ENVIRONMENT

The behavior of an individual with dementia is greatly influenced by the environment. Although pharmacological management is often required, environmental interventions are typically part of the long-term management plan as the two techniques together are the most effective way to minimize aggressive behavior. There are no fixed rules reagarding environmental management, but the model developed by Ryden and Feldt is particularly effective. Their model provided five specific goals of care, each of which speaks to an aspect of environmental management.

1. The person will feel safe. Skilled verbal and non-verbal communication with the person with dementia is critical to minimize fear and aggressive behavior. It is important that the care provider approaches the resident from the front and communication should commence with an introduction and some social chat so that trust can be built between the resident and the care provider. A calm voice and non-threatening body language are   critical to effective communication with the agitated or aggressive person.

2. The person will feel physically comfortable. In a person with dementia, pain presents as aggressive behavior. Persons with dementia are often unable to effectively communicate their needs. When the resident becomes very aggressive during procedures of care such as toileting, bathing etc. it is possible that there is a pain component. If there is pain associated with these tasks, it may be minimized through a combination of environmental and

pharmacological means; e.g. administration of analgesia prior to performing the care activity.

3. The person will experience a sense of control. As dementias progress, people progressively loose their independence and may, for the first time, become totally dependent on a care provider. This progressive loss of control over one's memory, finances, emotions, and physical needs is clearly frustrating to many people. This frustration and loss of personal control/power is often compounded by the introduction of new and unfamiliar caretakers. The combination can lead to aggression. It is very important to recognize the person's need to have some degree of control in situations and to avoid power struggles. If the resident refuses to carry out a certain task, it will be more fruitful for the care provider to leave the person and return a few minutes later to try again than to try to assert or force the issue. Also, wherever possible, it is important to give the resident choices that help them to regain a sense of control.

4. The person will experience an optimal level of stress. It has been established that both over and under stimulation are associated with agitation and aggression. Overstimulation can lead to behavioural disinhibition and aggression, as a well as a subjective sense of being overwhelmed. On the other hand, understimulation can also have a negative effect on the resident with dementia. Persons placed in very low stimulation environments – such as restraining chairs placed in quiet rooms often exhibit compensatory increases in repetitive and agitated behaviour. It is important to note that consistency in staffing and routines will go a long way towards minimizing aggressive behavior, presumably by allowing the person to achieve a state of equilibrium within the environment.

5. The person will experience pleasure. The demented resident will need to be engaged in activities appropriate for his or her level of functioning. It is important that the care provider becomes familiar with the interests of the resident as the activities could be organized to suit the individual's interests. Pleasurable activities do tend to displace aggressive behavior and can be one of the most effective tools in minimizing aggression in persons with dementia.

SUMMARY

In summary, agitation in the demented elderly population is a non-specific heterogeneous presentation that accompanies many physical and psychiatric disorders. Left untreated, agitation can lead to compromised physiological function and an increased risk for both morbidity and mortality. The short-term management of acute agitation/aggression is usually pharmacological, while the longer-term management must focus on the identification and treatment of the underlying illness. Effective long-term management must also include consideration of the environmental factors that may trigger or exacerbate agitated and aggressive behaviour.

REFERENCES

Drance E (1996) Aggresion in dementia: understanding the role of the physical and interpersonal environments *British Columbia Medical Journal.*, 38:10 pp 541-545

Rabins PV, Mace NL, Lucas MJ (1982) The impact of dementia on the family. *JAMA* , 248: 333-335.

Rapp MS, Flint AJ, Herrmann N, Proulx GB (1992). "Behavioral disturbances in the demented elderly: Phenomenology, pharmacotherapy and behavioral management", *Can J. Psychiatry* , 37: 651-657.

Reisberg B, Borenstein J, Salsb S, et al. (1987) Behavioral symptoms in Alzheimer's disease: Phenomenology and treatment, *J Clin Psychiatry,* 48:5 (Suppl): 9-15.

Ryden MB (1992) Alternatives to restraints and psychotropics in the care of aggressive cognitively impaired elderly persons, In: Buckwalter K (Ed). *Geriatric Mental Health Nursing: Current and future challenges.* Thorofare NJ: Slack Inc 84-93.

Weller PG, Mungus D, Bernick C (1988) Propranolol for the control of disruptive behaviour in senile dementia, *J. Geriatr. Psychiatry Neurol.*, 1: 266-230.

6

CLINICAL CONSIDERATIONS IN THE DIAGNOSIS AND MANAGEMENT OF GERIATRIC DELIRIUM

L.J. Sheldon

The observation that a variety of diseases and intoxicating substances can produce acute, global disruption of mind and behaviour is ancient. The use of the term *delirium* within medicine is more recent, dating to the 16th century. Since that time there have been many explanations of delirium, each placed with the prevailing theory of the time. Our current concept of delirium is based on the belief that the symptoms of delirium, regardless of the cause, are the result of acute, global, cerebral dysfunction. The symptoms the clinician looks for in establishing a diagnosis of dementia, disruption of basic cognitive processes (and particularly attentional capacities), a fluctuating level of consciousness, anxiety, agitation, delusions and hallucinations, are thought to be reflections of the general disruption of brain function.

This author traces the modern, North American, concept of delirium to the work of Adolph Meier. Meir coined the word *ergasia* to refer to the integration of biological, psychological, and social function in the context of the production of human behaviour. A state of ergasia, according to Meier, existed when the organism was in a state of health and fully functional. Although Meier did not speak to the issue of delirium, Wolf and Curran introduced the concept of "dysergastic reaction" to describe the general disruption of purposeful behaviour and disintegration of function that can occur in delirium.

With the introduction of the DSM diagnostic system, the diagnosis of delirium was standardized, at least within psychiatry. Although the DSM did not

Therapeutics in Geriatric Neuropsychiatry. Edited by R.J. Ancill, S.G. Holliday and A.H. Mithani. © 1997 John Wiley & Sons Ltd

necessarily retain the phenomenological richness of earlier work on delirium, it certainly provided an objective and standardized set of criteria for identifying and diagnosing delirium. It is a matter of debate whether the DSM system is fully adequate in terms of its identification of core symptoms of delirium as well as in terms of improving the specificity of the diagnosis.

More recently Lipowski has contributed to our understanding of delirium both in terms of basic clinical procedures for identifying and treating delirium, and in broadening the scope of practice to include the so-called "quiet deliriums" in which the symptom presented is less dominated by the florid symptoms of delusions, hallucinations, anxiety and agitation, than by the confusion, apathy, and related symptoms.

THE NATURAL HISTORY OF DELIRIUM

There are several epidemiological issues of which the clinician should be aware. First, the incidence of delirium dramatically increases after the age of 60. This is, no doubt, a direct result of the decreased physiological stability, increased occurrence of systemic disease, and increased use of medication that occurs in later life. Second, the incidence of occurrence of delirium is approximately equal in males and females.   Third, there seems to be no genetic predisposition to delirium, so all people are equally likely to develop this disorder. Fourth, a history of either brain injury or substance abuse is a marker for an increased likelihood of developing delirium.

Although delirium, in the majority of cases, is characterized by an acute onset, where it occurs against the pathological background of a dementia, the onset may be more insidious with the emergence of dysfunctional behavior being the clinical presentation. It is common for the clinical presentation to wax and wane over a 24 hour period and there may be brief periods of lucidity. Clinical lore holds that in cases of delirium there is a characteristic deterioration of function in the evening as sundown approaches. While this is less often the case in the geriatric patient, it does appear that the symptoms of a delirium become more pronounced when the patient is isolated in quiet or dark surroundings. While this is more likely at night, it will also be the case during the day if the patient is restricted to a sensory-deprived setting. Ironically, because of the modulating effect of sensory input on the behavioral expression of delirium, the patient is often more lucid and organized when the physician is present and carrying out an examination only to become florid when the physician leaves and the sensory input subsides. In most cases, once the underlying cause of the delirium is resolved, there is rapid resolution of symptoms, often within hours. However, where there are several contributing causes, the identification and treatment of one will not result in significant improvement and the clinician needs to keep seeking other pathological components.

While it is generally accepted that such florid symptoms as delusions and hallucinations are a part of the delirium syndrome, there are significant phenomenological differences when compared to the hallucinations and delusions associated with formal psychotic illness such as schizophrenia and mania. For example the hallucinations in delirium are predominantly visual or tactile and have a frightening quality. The delusions of delirium are rarely systematized and are usually fragmentary. It is the author's opinion, that these florid features should not be overemphasized when establishing the diagnosis, as they do not constitute the necessary and sufficient criteria for determining the presence of a delirium. In fact, the 'psychotic' phenomena of delirium are merely a reflection of global brain disturbance with similar fluctuation and disorganization as the cognitive disturbance.

The most valid diagnostic marker may well be the inability to maintain and shift attention. *Basic* attention processes tend to be fairly well maintained in depression, dementia, and psychosis, although there may be observed deficits on complex attention tasks. In delirium, on the other hand, there is almost always a marked reduction in performance on even the most simple attention tasks. Some simple bedside attention tasks are listed in Table 1.

Table 1. Simple Attention Tasks

Digit Repetition (Forward and Backwards) using 3-5 digit strings
Counting (Forwards and Backwards) from 1 to 10
Naming Days of the Week (Forward and Backward)
Naming Months of the Year (Forward and Backward)
Vigilance Tasks (Responding to a particular letter or word)

THE TWO-PART APPROACH TO THE MANAGEMENT OF DELIRIUM

The clinical management of delirium takes place in two stages. In the first stage, the clinician must ensure that the symptoms are sufficient to establish the syndromal diagnosis of delirium. At this stage, the emphasis is on determining that the presentation contains the core features of the disorder, manifested by attention deficits, and that competing diagnoses have been properly ruled out. The second stage involves establishing the etiological factors, thus defining the cause(s) of the delirium and consequently developing a therapeutic strategy.

In terms of the first stage, it is important to note that delirium is diagnosed on the basis of both the natural history of the disorder and cross-sectional presentation. In particular, the pattern of onset should be consistent with the normal course of a delirium, i.e. acute onset, rapid deterioration, fluctuating course and appropriate cognitive/behavioral symptoms. If the pattern differs, the onus is on the clinician to provide an adequate and convincing explanation, or to re-consider the diagnosis.

Completing the second stage of the management process can be challenging as establishing a correct etiologic diagnosis is not always easy. Firstly, there is a wide range of maladies that can cause a delirium. Delirium, like pyrexia, is a non-specific response of the brain to many conditions and, especially in the elderly, any illness or combination of pathological processes can produce a delirium. Although the causes of delirium, especially in the elderly, is a list as long as a list of possible diagnoses, some of the more common causes of delirium in the elderly are "drugs and bugs," that is, medications and infections, cardiac illness and stroke. Secondly, and this is particularly problematic in geriatric deliriums, is the problem of comorbidity. It is the experience of geriatric psychiatrists that most deliriums are multifactorial in that they are associated with several predisposing, precipitating, and perpetuating factors. Each of these factors will play a role in the development and resolution of a delirium. For example, an elderly person with decreased renal function and compromised cardio-vascular function has markedly decreased physiological capacity. These may predispose the person to the development of a delirium. The actual delirium may be precipitated by relatively minor acute infection that would not produce the same disturbance in an otherwise healthy individual. As the delirium develops, the person may decrease their fluid intake and, in doing so, perpetuate and exacerbate the delirium. In each case, the clinician must be aware of the need to identify and deal with each factor that impacts on the delirium.

Third, undisclosed substance abuse can complicate the diagnosis and treatment of a delirium. Substance abuse, especially alcohol or prescribed medications, in the geriatric population is more common than most people imagine. It becomes problematic if undetected as it can both precipitate and exacerbate deliriums. Determining the presence of substance abuse can be difficult as many elderly patients are reluctant to bring forward substance abuse problems and their family and caretakers may be unaware of the problem. The clinician, however, should make a point of looking for history or risk markers for substance abuse.

Once the etiologic diagnosis is established, the prognosis may be determined and specific interventions suggested. For example, an etiologic diagnosis of an *E. coli* urinary tract infection suggests a more favourable prognosis and points to a treatment using specific antibiotics   as determined by the clinician. Alternatively, a delirium determined to be caused by a brainstem infarct would suggest a poor prognosis, but might lead to the possibility of anti-embolic therapy.

THE DIFFERENTIAL DIAGNOSIS

From a psychiatric perspective, the differential diagnosis of delirium is a demanding task. In dealing with geriatric patients, the principal differentials are depression and dementia, although psychosis may also be a possible differential. An EEG may prove helpful if a good record can be obtained. In delirium, the EEG shows a characteristic pattern of *diffuse* low-amplitude fast activity, different from the fast activity seen with drugs such as the benzodiazepines which is more localized. However, delirium is an unlikely consequence of a psychiatric illness alone unless there is an organic etiology. This is the more common scenario in the elderly. What makes the differential diagnosis particularly challenging is that, in geriatric patients, there is considerable overlap of symptoms between the categories

Dementia can often be reliably differentiated from delirium on the basis of natural history. Dementia, and particularly Alzheimer's type dementias, are characterized by a slow and progressive loss of abilities that occurs over a period of months or years and is characterized by a lack of a return to a baseline level of function. While the cognitive and behavioural losses are global in nature, the loss is not severe and complete until the later stages of the disorder. This contrasts strongly with delirium where the typical course is rapid and symptom severity related to the underlying cause(s) and not time-dependent.

In the case of vascular dementias, and particularly in patients with significant vascular events, the onset may be rapid, but the overall course will be chronic and marked by progressive decline. While there may be some recovery of function, the overall trend will be toward more global impairment and decreased function. This contrasts strongly with delirium where the recovery of function is often substantial by the first day of treatment and there is a complete, or near-complete return to baseline function within a short time thereafter.

Differentiating depression form delirium is a more difficult problem, as geriatric depression can resemble delirium both symptomatically and in terms of its history. In recurrent depression, there is typically a series of discrete episodes, often occurring through adulthood. Each episode will be characterized by biological, psychological, and social impairment. In the later years, the psychological impairment can include both cognitive and behavioral dysfunction and in extreme cases the cognitive losses can be extensive.   It is also not uncommon to see a clinical picture that includes agitation and false beliefs.   Typically each episode is followed by recovery to baseline or near-baseline. On the face of it, then, there are strong similarities between geriatric depression (at least in some cases) and simple delirium.

Faced with this situation, the clinician must tread carefully. One important point of distinction between depression and delirium, and one which is of diagnostic value, is the rate of onset. A careful derived history of a depressive illness, and one which focuses on the prodromal features of depression, will often reveal a pattern of subacute onset. That is, the change in the person comes on gradually and is marked by pre-clinical signs and symptoms. This will contrast strongly with the acute onset typically seen in delirium. An exception to this general rule occurs in the case of the Levy Body variant of Alzheimer's disease where a slowly emerging delirium is often seen.

A careful review of the patient's psychiatric history will also help to differentiate depression from delirium.   Recurrent depression has a classic pattern of occurrence, remission, and relapse. Documenting such a pattern can establish the presence of depression and help to rule out a delirium. It is also important to determine if a diagnosis of dementia is part of the picture. In cases where there is a documented dementia, the clinician should look for a pattern of acute or subacute functional decline that is superimposed on the progressive and chronic decline of the dementia.   Unfortunately, this pattern of functional deterioration is, itself, indistinguishable from superimposed depression in dementia.

TREATMENT OF DELIRIUM

Management of delirium consists of two parallel treatment strategies: *supportive* therapy and *specific* therapy. Supportive measures are undertaken to improve or sustain basic biological function and are typically initiated immediately upon establishment of a syndromal diagnosis of delirium. Specific measures, on the other hand, are aimed at the actual cause of the delirium and should be initiated only after a presumptive etiologic diagnosis has been established.

Supportive measures can be required for biological, psychological, and environmental problems associated with the delirium. Basic biological support often includes provision of fluids, nutrients, and electrolytes to stabilize basic biological functions. It can also include establishment of mobility regimes and implementation of hygiene programs. The overall goal of biological support is to assure physical integrity and to re-establish physical stability. Psychological support can include the management of delusions and hallucinations, as well as control of agitation and aggressive behaviour. These supportive measures may be either pharmacological or behavioural. If one-to-one nursing care is available this can be a very effective means of managing the delirious patient. Many delirious patients will calm down to a substantial extent in the presence of other people and the presence of a calm, skilled nurse can help to contain a difficult situation. (Parenthetically, as mentioned earlier, the examining clinician should be aware that his/her presence may also have a calming effect on the patient and may actually lead the clinician to underestimate the severity of the problem). Pharmacological treatment, however, may be the only realistic management option. If substance withdrawal is suspected, the prescribing of cross-tolerated substances can often lead to rapid settling of hallucinations. While there is no fixed rule, small doses of neuroleptics are generally effective when used to treat symptoms of delirium.

Environmental supports and modifications can dramatically effect hallucinations, delusions, and behavioral dysfunction. Delirious patients are particularly sensitive to the physical and social environment. They are generally unable to tolerate high intensity stimulation and rapid environmental changes. Consequently, providing adequate light (to reduce shadows and contrasts), limiting the intensity of stimulation (turn off commercial radio stations and televisions, removing the person from noisy environments, etc.) and avoiding rapidly changing stimulus situations (people coming and going, several people talking at once) will have a beneficial effect on all aspects of the delirious presentation including delusions, hallucinations, and agitation. However, as stated earlier, too low a level of external stimulation will lead to an emergence of the patient's internal cognitive chaos.   It is extremely important to realize that the solution to the problem of sensitivity to the environment is NOT to put the delirious patient in a traditional quiet area such as an isolation room. It is very clear that the delirious patient can no better tolerate a sensorily restricted environment than they can an overly stimulating one. What seems to be the most effective strategy is to keep the person in an environment with a moderate degree of controlled stimulation and avoiding any type of over-stimulation.

Specific corrective interventions, of course, are directed at the cause(s) of the delirium. Given the extensive list of possible cause, it is of no value to discuss specific interventions. The clinician, when choosing an intervention, should keep in mind that most pharmacological interventions carry with them the possibility of toxicity and delirium.   The clinician's choice of a particular intervention will be more effective if it is based on a careful consideration of the tolerability of the treatment and guided by a principle of choosing, whenever possible, the least potentially toxic substance. Following initiation of therapy, the clinician should be particularly alert to the emergence of both serious and minor side effects, particularly if the patient, as a result of the delirium, has a further decreased physiological capacity.

MONITORING THE CLINICAL COURSE OF A DELIRIUM

Once a diagnosis of delirium has been established, supportive measures put in place, and specific treatments initiated, the clinician must monitor for signs of improvement.   Clinical lore suggests that the 72 hours subsequent to the initiation of specific treatments are crucial, and that resolutions should be expected following that period. It is the opinion of the author that there are several subtle patterns of change that can occur during the early stages of treatment - patterns that can predict the overall course and outcome.

The fist prognostic pattern to look for is a change in level of consciousness. In the author's experience, the degree to which the level of consciousness is reduced is related to the degree of impairment of critical organs or organ systems. It is reasonable to assume than an improving level of consciousness indicates an improvement in the underlying pathology. Thus, the improvement in level of consciousness early in the stages of treatment is likely to suggest a favourable trend toward recovery.

The second pattern to look for is a change in the nature of the psychological impairment associated with the delirium. By definition, delirium consists of global cognitive impairment. As the delirium resolves, there may be recovery of some aspects of function prior to full return to baseline. For example, an isolated improvement in orientation may well herald a trend to overall improvement. Similarly, improved verbal output, and changes in praxis may be signs of the beginning of a trend to recovery.

THE QUESTION OF CHRONIC DELIRIUM

Chronic delirium was, until recently, a relatively uncommon diagnosis. Even in cases of apparently chronic delirium, such as those associated with auto-immune vasculitis or neuritis, there is some question as to whether the delirium is truly persistent over time. In the author's experience, the delirium associated with such conditions is not truly chronic. Rather, it is a series of discrete episodes, although the episodes may have temporal contiguity. It appears to be likely that in these cases the situation is defined by the presence of intermittent precipitating or perpetuating factors, rather than by chronic delirium.

Since introduction of the diagnosis of the Levy Body variant of Alzheimer's disease, the diagnosis of chronic delirium has been more common. From a clinical perspective, this appears to be a true chronic delirium that is caused by the disease. Unfortunately, this type of delirium is largely intractable. The supportive measures described above, and particularly the psychological and environmental interventions, can help to reduce the degree of observable dysfunction. The use of specific behavior management techniques may also be an option, although such a discussion is beyond the scope of this chapter.

PREVENTION OF GERIATRIC DELIRIUM

There are a number of simple, common-sense measures that can be used to help to prevent the occurrence of geriatric delirium. The most important is maintaining general health. Regular examination by a physician to detect systemic and acute disorders that can precipitate delirium and to monitor and adjust medications are of key importance. Control of drinking and the use of non-prescription medications is also a part of this picture. In terms of life-style factors, it seems clear that proper nutrition, proper rest, and regular exercise leave the person with better physiological capabilities and, in consequence, a reduced risk to develop delirium.

Aging is certainly not without problems, and when chronic disease occurs, carefully chosen treatment and proper follow-up are essential to reduce the occurrence of toxicity, and disease-related delirium. Because many drugs carry a risk for delirium in the elderly patient, as noted above the choice of treatment for both acute and chronic disease is of paramount importance.

The overall thrust of prevention, in short, is to keep the elderly patient at the highest level of health and in their most robust physical state. This includes proper medical care and life-style management. It also includes individual analysis and identification of pre-disposing factors with appropriate action when necessary.

SUMMARY

Delirium is a common but not inevitable problem in geriatrics. Proper preventive action will also help to reduce the rate of occurrence. Proper practice patterns, good diagnostic techniques, sound therapeutic practice, and good monitoring will ensure that delirium will be quickly identified and treated. The clinician should remain optimistic recognizing that the vast majority of persons with delirium can be vigorously and successfully treated.

SUGGESTED READING

Lipowski ZJ (1990) Delirium (Acute Confusional States)In: *Principles of Geriatric Medicine and Gerontology*, 2nd Edition Eds: Hazzard WR, Andres R, Bierman EL & Blass JPMcGraw Hill Inc.

Beresin EV (1988) Delirium in the Elderly. *Journal of Geriatric Psychiatry and Neurology*, 1, 127

Mori E & Yamadori A (1987) Acute Confusional State and Acute Agitated Delirium. *Archives of Neurology*, 44, 1139

Gambert, S (1992) Substance Abuse in the Elderly In: *Substance Abuse: A Comprehensive Textbook*, 2nd Edition Eds: Lowinson JH, Ruiz P & Millman RB Williams & Wilkins

7

CHRONIC PAIN IN THE ELDERLY – A PSYCHIATRIC SYNDROME?

Raymond J. Ancill

Providing effective treatment to individuals whose pain complaints are disproportionate to their demonstrable pathology, who respond poorly to physical treatment, and whose pain complaints endure in time is a challenge to clinicians. From a psychiatric perspective, it is important to look for a specific type of pain – pain that is likely to respond to psychiatric treatment. It is my experience that elderly patients who present with long-term complaints of chronic pain are among the most challenging to be seen in geriatric psychiatry. The complexity in dealing with pain in this population is related both to the nature of the chronic pain syndrome and the nature of aging. In younger patients, it is often relatively easy to determine if a pain complaint has a significant organic basis and either the presence or absence of chronic systemic disease (i.e. rheumatoid arthritis) will likely be diagnostic. The geriatric patient tends to be more complex. Age-associated illnesses such as osteoarthritis, osteoporosis, cardiac disease and other degenerative disorders carry with them considerable discomfort and make it difficult to determine if an elderly patient's complaints are disproportionate to their physical state.

The clinician dealing with the geriatric patient may find himself facing a dilemma: Should the pain complaints be deemed to be appropriate to the physical state, or written off to some other cause. This is not an easy call. Clearly, much pain in the elderly is "chronic" in the sense that it continues over time. But, equally clearly, most people do a remarkable job of living with that

Therapeutics in Geriatric Neuropsychiatry. Edited by R.J. Ancill, S.G. Holliday and A.H. Mithani. © 1997 John Wiley & Sons Ltd

pain. Is a complaining patient being realistic or histrionic and malingering? Should the intervention be physical or psychiatric?

Many physicians feel that they can quickly and accurately identify their "chronic pain patients." It is often the case, however, that the label "chronic pain patient" merely describes patients who frequently appear at doctors' offices and who fail to respond to an array of analgesic treatments. The situation in which patients fail to respond to treatment and continue to present with the same complaint is clearly frustrating to both the patient and physician. And given this type of situation it is understandable why these patients often find themselves in a perpetual motion of referral and ineffective treatment. Occasionally, and typically quite late in the process, a psychiatric referral is sought–usually out of desperation. This situation is unfortunate because, as I will argue, a psychiatric assessment and treatment can be the key to solving these cases.

Before examining the psychiatric perspective on the diagnosis and treatment of chronic pain syndrome, it is worth reviewing a psychiatric model of pain syndromes. In my opinion, pain syndromes can be subdivided into three distinct groups: acute pain syndromes, persistent pain syndromes, and chronic pain syndromes. In the younger patient it is usually possible to differentiate these syndromes, as pain in younger people typically contrasts strongly with a background of generally good health. In the elderly, when acute and systemic illnesses are a predictable feature of the background, distinguishing between the three syndromes becomes more difficult and, in fact, all three can coexist in a single patient. However, discriminating among these syndromes is the *sine qua non* of pain management and, conversely, failing to do so often results in the creation of a refractory patient who is exposed to far too many inappropriate treatments. A brief description of each syndrome appears below.

ACUTE PAIN

Acute pain is generally caused by an acute inflammatory response to an identified agent or precipitant. Swelling and visible signs of insult typically accompany it. Acute pain responds to analgesics and anti-inflammatories and, in many cases will resolve without significant sequelae. It is rarely associated with emergent psychiatric symptoms.

PERSISTENT PAIN

Persistent pain is caused by a long-term structural change that is associated with a significant insult or injury. There is often an observable functional deficit and the structural change can usually be visualized or otherwise measured using conventional methodologies. Persistent pain may respond only partially to analgesics and anti-inflammatories, as the pain is consequent to the change in structure rather than to an inflammatory response. The clinician should be aware, however, that there are many circumstances in which elements of both persistent and acute pain can be found. Psychiatric features may emerge if the persistent pain is long-standing or severe but these tend to be reactive in nature and often appropriate to the objective level of discomfort or dysfunction.

CHRONIC PAIN

Chronic pain steadily occurs over an extended period of time and its main feature is that it does not respond to analgesia. The exception to this is neuropathic pain (thalamic syndromes, phantom-limb pain) where there is both a known physical cause for the pain and a coherent medical explanation of non-responsiveness. The syndrome of chronic pain is characterized by the patient's phenomenological accounts of the pain, which ten to be extreme, dramatic, incongruent and incompatible with any observable pathology. It is worthy of note that patients who complain of chronic pain, especially the elderly, invariably refer to a site of current or previous injury or surgery. Although there is seldom any indication of current pathology, these reports both suggest that there may have once been some organic basis for the complaint and raise the suspicion that learned behaviour patterns play a part in the situation. Despite proven histories of non-responsiveness, these patients are often on large numbers of potent and toxic narcotics and nonsteroidal anti-inflammatories. This suggests that many physicians continue to prescribe pain medications and only reluctantly stop them. Sadly, chronic pain patients often develop both a physiological and psychological dependence on narcotics and are subsequently, and unfairly, labeled as "substance abusers."

TREATING PAIN COMPLAINTS

Clearly, the first step in diagnosing and treating chronic pain syndrome is excluding the possibility of acute or persistent pain. If physical and laboratory reports are inconclusive regarding an etiological factor, it is important to determine if the pain can be controlled with analgesics. Perhaps the underrated analgesic is plain acetaminophen. It is my experience that acetominophen is rarely prescribed or taken appropriately and reports of lack of efficacy should be closely examined. The most effective regime with geriatric patients is two tablets every three hours while awake. This is generally sufficient to deal with inflammatory reactions. If a response is adequate but there is breakthrough pain, a *prn* of a narcotic such as codeine or morphine at a low dose can be effective. Less potent nonsteroidals, such as nabumetone or ibuprofen, can also be helpful *in the presence of an acute inflammatory reaction.* However, the elderly remain exquisitely sensitive to the side effects of nonsteroidal drugs especially gastrointestinal bleeding.

If the patient does not respond to analgesics, a diagnosis of chronic pain syndrome should be considered. The clinician should keep in mind these three points: 1. True chronic pain has little to do with actual pain, either acute or persistent. 2. True chronic pain is reflective of an abnormal mental state. 3. There may actually be co-morbid acute or persistent pain elements in the presentation. The abnormal mental state that characterizes chronic pain syndrome is dramatically illustrated in the following clinical case:

> *The patient, a 72 year old woman, was admitted to a geriatric psychiatry inpatient unit. On examination she was fully oriented with no apparent cognitive deficits. She was neatly dressed, well-groomed and exhibited appropriate social skills.*
>
> *When asked why she was in hospital she stated that it was to cure her intractable and unbearable pain. When asked to rate the pain she claimed that on a scale of 1 to 10 the pain was "at least 15," and the worst pain she could ever imagine experiencing. While providing this description she sat calmly in a chair with relaxed muscle tone and responsive facial movements. She also provided a temporal account of the pain which stated that the pain remained at the same level 24 hours a day, never varied in intensity, was not amenable to distraction, relaxation, medication, or any other management technique. Later in the interview, when asked to discuss her mood, she claimed that the pain was now worse than it had ever been and that she thought that she might actually be dying. This was presented in a calm voice with no sign of distress.*
>
> *By history and presentation, a diagnosis of depression was established and she was eventually treated with a course of*

ECT. By the end of the treatment, the pain complaints had greatly diminished, although they did not entirely disappear, and her overall level of function improved greatly. Approximately one year later she experienced a relapse and the pain complaints re-emerged. A second course of ECT was administered with a successful outcome.

The above case illustrates that while the pain complaints of the chronic pain syndrome patient are not all in the mind (at least in the sense of being imagined or made up) they can certainly be indicative of an abnormal mental state. The case outlined above also illustrates an important point, chronic pain more commonly occurs within the context of serious and chronic mood disorders, usually depression.

In the case of co-morbid chronic pain and depression, it is important to emphasize that aggressive treatment with well-tolerated antidepressants is a major component of the management of chronic pain syndrome. The depression in many of these cases, however, is often quite refractory to standard therapies and higher doses, combinations of agents or ECT is often required, as in the above case.

A second vignette illustrates the co-morbid presentation of delusions and chronic pain syndrome.

A 68 year old female presented as an outpatient to a geriatric psychiatry outpatient clinic with a three-year history of what she described as "unrelenting agony." The family physician had sent excellent and detailed notes concerning her history. There was no physical cause associated with her complaint and she had failed many courses of analgesia and other interventions and was somewhat ambivalent about seeing a psychiatrist. On the one hand she felt "desperate" and would see anyone who might be able to help but, on the other hand, she was quite affronted that anyone might feel that her pain was all in her mind.

On arriving for her appointment she was noted to be elegantly dressed, properly made up and cooperative and compliant during the interview. Good rapport was easily established and she was both articulate and intelligent. At one point during the interview, the patient stated that I clearly did not appreciate how much agony she was in. In order to explore this, knowing that she had three children born vaginally, I asked her to compare the pain she was feeling at that precise moment with childbirth. She told me that this current pain was "much, much worse." While telling me this, she was calmly sitting in a chair with her legs gracefully crossed with no sign of either physical or psychological distress.

Given the lack of an identifiable cause of the pain, a history of non-responsiveness to analgesics, and strong evidence of an abnormal mental state, a diagnosis of chronic pain syndrome was established. Since her description of her pain was incongruent with her affect and behaviour, and since she was unwilling to entertain any serious discussion that questioned her report, she was determined to be holding a fixed and false belief – a form of delusion. Given this presentation, treatment with risperidone, an antipsychotic, was initiated. Over the course of the next few weeks, her complaint diminished considerably and follow-up over the next six months showed no recurrence.

The clinician must be vigilant for the patient whose complaints of chronic pain are a somatic delusion associated with an affective psychosis and consider antipsychotic medications. These medications must be used with care. The more traditional neuroleptics, such as chlorpromazine or haloperidol, are associated with significant levels of toxicity, both acute and chronic. This will result in poor patient compliance or, conversely, incorporation of any emergent adverse events into the syndrome itself. Currently, the most appropriate choices for an antipsychotic in this situation would be risperidone or olanzepine. Risperidone is a serotonergic antipsychotic which is well-tolerated by the elderly. Initial dosing is 0.5mg at night rising to a usual maintenance of 2 – 3 mg per day either as a single nighttime dose or divided BID. Olanzepine appears to be more useful in resistant cases and doses start at 2.5 mg once a day for the elderly with a maintenance dose of 10 – 20 mg per day. Any residual acute or persistent pain elements must also be aggressively managed as discussed earlier.

The final aspect of chronic pain treatment is the psychological component. From a psychological perspective, the patient with chronic pain syndrome generally exhibits maladaptive and dysfunctional patterns of thought and behaviour. This is somewhat predictable, as in many cases "pain" has virtually taken over the patients' lives and their whole existence may revolve around visits to physicians, therapists, and pain clinics. At home, it is not uncommon to find that the lives of family members are largely preoccupied with the needs of the pain patient. If the patient is married, it is common to find significant marital disharmony although it is not clear whether this is a cause or an effect of the chronic pain situation. The patients' preoccupation with pain also leads them to seek out anyone who is either willing to listen to them or who offers them help. This leaves the patient especially vulnerable to the "alternative medicine" industry whom, in my experience, have no more success than the more "traditional" practitioners in dealing with chronic pain syndrome.

In many cases, these patients can benefit from supportive psychotherapy, although it is not easily available and rarely offered. It is important to note that the problems presented by the chronic pain patient often have nothing to do with pain per se. Consequently, the traditional psychological techniques offered for the treatment/management of pain are not indicated. In fact, it there is a suspicion of psychosis; such procedures as deep muscle relaxation and guided imagery are clearly contra-indicated.

The focus of therapy in cases of chronic pain syndrome is two-phase. In the first phase, the emphasis is on identifying cognitive errors or areas of personal dysfunction that are part of the chronic pain syndrome. The goal is to use traditional techniques such as cognitive restructuring to help the person to achieve a more stable level of intra-personal function.

The second phase is the identification and changing of the pain-centered lifestyle. As noted earlier, many chronic pain patients develop life and social styles that are centered entirely on pain. Identification and elimination of secondary gains, development of new response contingencies – particularly on the part of family and caregivers – and the gradual introduction of a more balanced life-style are generally the goals of this phase. An important part of this is working with family members and caregivers who must be taught appropriate responses to pain complaints and supported in their efforts to change their roles in a pain-centered life-style.

In closing, there are two more issues to be considered. The first is the need for timely and effective psychiatric evaluation. In the early stages of the syndrome, the patient seldom have a comprehensive evaluation, and the assessment will likely focus exclusively on the "pain," A psychiatric assessment, if it is requested at all, will occur only late in the course of the illness. This is extremely problematic as it is unclear whether the refractory nature of chronic pain syndrome is an inherent quality of the illness or a phenomenon of chronicity and late intervention. And, unfortunately, it is often the case that by the time a psychiatrist is involved, the patient may have much difficulty in giving up the 'disease' lifestyle and for these patients the long-term prognosis may be poor. Fortunately, the majority of patients are not impervious to treatment and will show significant improvement if the clinician is patient and persistent.

The final issue to consider is that chronic pain syndrome may occur in the context of litigation. Insurance companies and the Workers Compensation Boards are inundated with people who complain of chronic pain in spite of no independent observable pathology to account for it. Some of these claimants have a Chronic Pain Syndrome as described earlier, but many are malingering and have no reason to "get better". Unfortunately, the time required discriminating between the genuine and the fraudulent is often not taken and even patients with demonstrable pathology are treated as if they are attempting to perpetuate a fraud. The clinician needs to be aware of the social context in which the complaint is occurring and to be careful to base the clinical diagnosis on solid ground. Identifying the abnormal mental state is again the key. It is certainly true that the precipitating event in the genesis of a chronic pain syndrome can be an automobile or work-related injury, but this is unusual. Often what is put forward as the "cause" by the patient is incompatible with the extent of the subsequent level of complaint or dysfunction.

In conclusion, Chronic Pain Syndrome is a complex yet common problem that can have an unremitting and destructive effect on the life of the patient. Many of patients with Chronic Pain Syndrome are elderly and the task of accurately assessing and treating them can be difficult. But while the challenges are great, diligent clinical work will often reap significant reward for both patient and doctor.

8

ELECTROCONVULSIVE THERAPY IN DEMENTIA

L. Myronuk, M. Illing & M.Geizer

INTRODUCTION

Electroconvulsive therapy has long been recognised as a highly effective treatment for a number of psychiatric and neuropsychiatric conditions. First introduced by Cerletti in 1938 (Colp, 1996), electroconvulsive therapy (ECT) is the induction of a grand-mal seizure via the application of electrical stimulation to the brain. Traditionally thought of as a last-resort therapeutic option, refinements in knowledge about its mode of action, improved stimulus delivery techniques, and a growing literature on efficacy have led to its use as a secondary or primary treatment option in patients who are acutely ill and either non-responsive or adversely sensitive to pharmacological interventions. A variety of psychiatric (Hay, 1996) and neuropsychiatric (Zwil and Pelchat, 1994) conditions have been shown to be responsive to ECT, although mood disorders and particularly depression remain the most common indication for ECT. Jenike (1989) found ECT to be used more often in the elderly, because depressions are more likely to be severe; and because of increased likelihood of concurrent medical illnesses where anticholinergic, cardiotoxic or hypotensive effects of antidepressant medications would be undesirable. With contemporary techniques, the mortality rate reported for ECT is 2/100,000 treatments (Abrams, 1991), no higher than that reported for general anaesthesia alone (Inglis and Farnill, 1993).

At this point, there is little to debate about whether or not ECT is a legitimate treatment option. In the case of the elderly, where medical conditions such as

Therapeutics in Geriatric Neuropsychiatry. Edited by R.J. Ancill, S.G. Holliday and A.H. Mithani. © 1997 John Wiley & Sons Ltd

chronic hypotension, cardio-vascular disease, and other systemic disorders make pharmacological treatment problematic, ECT is not only often indicated, but may be the only available choice for treatment. The use of ECT in the elderly person suffering from comorbid dementia and depression has been the focus of considerable discussion and research in recent years (see, for example, Lam, 1990). The consensus that seems to be emerging is that there is no inherent contraindication to the use of ECT when a person is demented with depressive symptomatology, and is not a good candidate for pharmacological therapy. The following sections of this chapter identify the cases in which ECT is a legitimate treatment option for the person with dementia, and discusses both efficacy and side effects issues, as well as the procedures for administering ECT.

ECT-RESPONSIVE CONDITIONS ASSOCIATED WITH DEMENTIA

ALZHEIMER'S DISEASE

Alzheimer's disease is the most common form of dementia, accounting for at least 60% of all documented instances of dementia. Depressive symptoms have been reported in up to 87% of patients with Alzheimer type dementia, with frank suicidal thoughts occurring in up to 20% of these cases (Gottfries, 1996). ECT can be effective in treating depression occurring during Alzheimer type dementia, regardless of whether or not there is a history of recurrent major depressive disorder prior to the development of the dementia. The literature also suggests that administration of ECT can lead to improvement of the psychotically depressed demented patient when antidepressant medication has previously caused deterioration (Snow and Wells, 1981). Treatment of depression in dementia is easily justified by the significant symptomatic relief that can be achieved, as well as reduced burden on caregivers (Snow & Wells, 1981).

MANIA

Between 3% and 17% percent of patients with Alzheimer type dementia will manifest symptoms of mania (McGuire and Rabins, 1994). Mania will also respond to ECT, even though a transient elevation of mood may be induced by the ECT (Small et al., 1991).

AGITATION

Agitation is one of the common modes of presentation for depressive syndromes in the elderly demented patient. In some cases, dementia that is far-advanced will have a clinical manifestation that includes severe agitation, with palilalia or aggression. The severity of cognitive impairment may preclude ascertainment of sufficient criteria to formally establish the presence of a full major depressive syndrome. However, a clinical diagnosis can be established by a properly trained physician and ECT may still produce significant clinical improvement when used judiciously with this group (Carlyle et al., 1991).

PARKINSON'S DISEASE

At least 50% of patients with Parkinson's disease become depressed at some point during their illness, with as many as one third having depression present at the time of their diagnosis (Koller and Megaffin, 1994; Calne and Calne, 1997). Our experience is that first onset of a depressive illness in late life will frequently herald the onset within several months to years of either Parkinson's disease, or some other progressive deteriorating condition affecting subcortical structures. Patients with Parkinson's disease may be particularly suited to treatment with ECT, as it has the capacity not only to improve mood symptoms, but also the movement disorder and the psychotic side effects of dopaminomimetic therapy (see below). Mania occurring in the context of Parkinson's disease can also be expected to respond favourably to ECT (Atre-Vaidya and Jampala, 1988).

The effect of ECT on the symptoms of Parkinson's disease was noted above but deserves further comment. ECT has been shown to improve the motor symptoms and bradyphrenia of Parkinson's disease (Rasmussen and Abrams, 1991), leading to reduction in requirements for prodopaminergic medications. Even manifestations of severe disease, such as "on-off" phenomena, may be improved (Burke et al., 1988). There is evidence that the ECT is acting directly to ameliorate extrapyramidal symptoms, rather than indirectly via improvement of depression: Burke's group (1988) observed a dissociation between the rate and timing of response for mood symptoms compared to motor symptoms. Movement can show improvement with no detectable change in mood or cognition (Young et al., 1985).

While spontaneous psychosis occurring as a part of Parkinson's disease is thought to be rare, psychotic symptoms produced by dopaminomimetic and anticholinergic antiparkinsonian agents are common (Koller and Megaffin, 1994). Delusions, hallucinations (with or without insight) and confusion all may be seen. While the usual approach would be to reduce the offending medication(s), at least for some patients this can lead to immobility that may be life-threatening. Psychotic symptoms may respond to ECT, whether used alone

(Factor et al., 1995b; Hurwitz et al., 1988), or in combination with non-parkinsonising antipsychotic medications such as clozapine (Factor et al, 1995a).

HUNTINGTON'S DISEASE

Mood disorders occur in approximately 40% of patients diagnosed with Huntington's disease, with a 3:1 ratio of depressed to mixed presentations (McGuire and Rabins, 1994). In two thirds of Huntington's patients, the mood syndrome will antedate the movement disorder or the emergence of dementia (Lishman, 1987). ECT has been used successfully to treat mood disorder in the setting of Huntington's disease (Zwil and Pelchat, 1994), but has not been shown to be superior to conventional pharmacological treatments in this population (McGuire & Rabins, 1994).

VASCULAR DEMENTIAS

Twenty-five to fifty percent of elderly patients will manifest a depressive disorder following stroke (Starkenstein and Robinson, 1994). The greatest risk for depression is following stroke to the dominant frontal region (Reichman, 1996), although depression can follow a CVA involving any brain region. While a recent or evolving stroke is a relative contraindication for ECT (Zwil and Pelchat, 1994), ECT can be safely administered without special modification once the neurological injury has stabilised (Murray et al., 1986). Poststroke depression responds favourably to ECT (Abrams, 1991), and can also impact favourably on both comorbid cognitive impairment and delusions (Murray et al., 1986). Pain related to thalamic infarction has been reported to improve during ECT for poststroke depression as well (Murray et al., 1986).

Poststroke mania is less commonly observed, but can be associated with nondominant or bifrontal lesions (Starkenstein and Robinson, 1994). More commonly, a manic picture is seen in a stroke patient who is being treated for depression, and has a transient mood-state switch induced by antidepressant therapy. The management of treatment-emergent mania is beyond the scope of this chapter, but when this abrupt mood change is seen during a course of ECT, we have found that it is often possible to continue with the course and "treat through" the mania. Patients being treated for mania will respond to ECT at a rate similar to that for depressed patients (Small et al., 1991).

The recent advent of accessible neuroimaging technologies has made antemortem diagnosis of abnormalities deep in the brain's white matter and subcortical nuclei possible. Ischemic demyelination (*leukoencephalopathy*) can be detected with CT scanning, but is generally more apparent with MRI (Coffey et al., 1988). Coffey and colleagues (1988) found that two thirds of their elderly depressed patients going for ECT had radiographic evidence of leukoencephalopathy. Interestingly, their patients showing leukoencephalopathy had good or excellent responses to ECT in 98% of cases.

ECT AS A TREATMENT PROBE

As dementias progress, patients steadily lose cognitive and behavioural capacity. As patients' repertoires narrow, their responses may cease to be stimulus-specific: crying out or palilalia may indicate pain, hunger, boredom, anxiety, nausea, sadness, or some other state. When the severely demented patient is unable to communicate his or her state any more clearly, the clinician must weigh the cost of allowing the patient to remain distressed against the potential risks and benefits of a course of treatment. In such a setting, we will consider using a brief course of empiric ECT as a probe, to determine if there is a treatment-responsive mood component to their presentation.

ECT AND COGNITIVE IMPAIRMENT

The fear of cognitive dysfunction in general and memory loss in particular is the legacy of the early uses, and misuses, of ECT. Writing in 1991, Shapira et al. noted that, "Cognitive dysfunction, particularly memory impairment, is the only adverse effect of ECT that poses a significant problem in clinical practice" (Shapira et a.l, 1991, p.938). The possibility of cognitive impairment was traditionally seen as particularly problematic if the patient had a pre-existing brain disorder. In fact, earlier in this century, it was considered contraindicated to administer ECT to patients with cerebral lesions (Smith et al., 1942). The prevailing belief at that time was that the use of ECT would not only worsen the patient's immediate mental condition, but would lead to a hastening of the course of a dementia. Fortunately, and as we will discuss, the problem of cognitive side-effects is much less serious than has been traditionally believed. The following discussion examines the literature on the adverse cognitive effects of ECT with the goal of helping the clinician to assess the effect of ECT on patients with cognitive difficulties.

ADVERSE COGNITIVE EFFECTS OF ECT – GENERAL ISSUES

Adverse cognitive effects that have been reported to occur with ECT treatment include memory impairment, delirium, and general cognitive deterioration. While it was initially thought that these side-effects were primarily attributable to the ECT itself, it is now known that effects also associated with the anaesthesia process that is part of the operative procedure. The adverse cognitive effects associated with general anaesthetic are described elsewhere (Tzabar et al, 1996; Williams-Russo et al, 1995). This discussion will focus only on effects directly attributable to the ECT itself.

MEMORY IMPAIRMENT

Grand mal seizures, whether spontaneous or induced, are associated with an interval of post-ictal confusion that is characterised by deficits in short-term memory (Mendez, 1996; Hay, 1996). It is also common for some disorientation to occur while the patient is recovering from anaesthesia, but for most patients this clears after approximately two hours. More subtle abnormalities of neuropsychological function may persist for days, including mild disturbances of new learning/short-term memory skills and attention/concentration abilities. Where there is pre-existing dementia or encephalopathy, a higher incidence of post-ECT confusion is seen (Zwil and Pelchat, 1994). Cognition typically returns to the pre-ECT level by one month after treatment, and has been reported to be significantly better than baseline at 6 months (Shapira et al., 1991; Small et al., 1991; Zwil & Pelchat, 1994), even in patients with structural brain pathology (Murray et al., 1986).

If successive treatments are administered without adequate clearing of cognitive function, cumulative effects can build across the course of treatments (Weiner, 1982). Clinically, this manifests as increasing memory impairment (Shapira et al, 1991) or decreased functional capacity (Regestein et al., 1975). Fortunately, our experience parallels that of others: "...in our experience, cognitive function is unchanged or improved even after bilateral ECT treatment" (p.283, Liang et al., 1988)

DELIRIUM

Delirium (fluctuating orientation, decreased attention and global impairment in cognitive function) occasionally appears after several ECT treatments have been administered. Delirium has been understood to be a cumulative effect from the series of treatments. Advancing age brings alterations in blood-brain barrier (BBB) permeability and in metabolic clearance of drugs (Morley, 1996). When combined with the further increase in BBB permeability produced by ECT (Bergsholm et al., 1989), these changes set the stage for CNS accumulation of compounds and associated widespread disturbances of cerebral function. Management of the patient with emergent delirium during ECT includes both supportive measures, including judicious use of tranquillisation where necessary, as well as modification to the ECT schedule (more allowance for recovery between successive sessions) or technique (unilateral treatments in lieu of bilateral).

Likely because of the deliria encountered that arise from ECT, many clinicians in the UK and North America would not treat an acutely delirious patient with ECT. In Scandinavia, however, ECT has frequently been used with success in the management of the delirious patient (Dubovsky, 1986). In their recent review, Zwil and Pelchat (1994) concluded, "In cases where agitation secondary to organic delirium presents a significant management problem or obstructs medical treatment, alleviation of delirium with ECT may allow more effective treatment of the causative disorder. In those conditions, like NMS and delirium tremens, in which the delirium itself carries a significant potential for morbidity and mortality, the early use of ECT may be life-saving" (p. 13).

ADMINISTERING ECT TO THE PATIENT WITH DEMENTIA

CONTRAINDICATIONS

With refinements in ECT and anaesthetic techniques, it was found that patients with dementias and other brain pathologies could tolerate and benefit from ECT, without causing deterioration of their neurological status (Benbow, 1988; Lam, 1990). Most recent reviews conclude that there are no absolute contraindications to ECT. Some conditions require special attention: increased intracranial pressure, cerebral aneurysm, recent CVA or head trauma, and active CNS infection (Zwil and Pelchat, 1994).

FREQUENCY AND DURATION OF TREATMENT

In the review of Shapira et al., (1991), it was reported that twice weekly ECT was the norm within the UK, and that in North America treatments were usually administered three times weekly. Differences were found in the rates of cognitive side effects of treatment, with shorter treatment intervals more strongly associated with side-effects, especially for elderly patients receiving bilateral ECT. No difference was found in the efficacy between two- and three-times-per-week treatment (Lerer et al., 1995). Patients treated three times weekly did receive more total treatments, however, and generally showed improvement in target symptoms more quickly.

Dubovsky (1986) recommended administering the same number of ECT in a course of treatment to those with mood disorder and neurological condition, as would be given to those with mood disorder alone. In our experience, patients with late-life onset of mood symptoms arising in the context of neurological disease respond more quickly to treatment than do those patients with life-long histories of recurrent primary mood disorder. We agree with Shapira and colleagues' (1991) recommendation that, "Cessation of treatment should thus be dictated by the patient's clinical condition and not by whether an arbitrary criterion regarding number of treatments has been reached" (p.945).

STIMULUS PARAMETERS

During a course of ECT, parameters are generally based on the observed response to the antecedent treatment. Setting the parameters for the first treatment in a series requires some other technique, and two methods have been advocated. The individual patient's seizure threshold can be determined empirically, by starting with subthreshold stimuli and successively increasing the parameters during the same anaesthetic and restimulating until a seizure is obtained. While this technique may be preferred for treatment of younger individuals, in elderly or cardiac-compromised patients these subconvulsive stimuli should be avoided, because vagal parasympathetic outflow from the stimulation will be unopposed by the sympathetic discharge of seizure (Zwil & Pelchat, 1994). An alternative is to choose settings based on population seizure thresholds, with reference to the patient's age and gender. The elderly typically need high stimulus intensity (Weiner, 1982), but the wide range of seizure thresholds even in the elderly means that using population-based parameters will expose some patients to more stimulus energy than they require.

STIMULUS ADMINISTRATION

There has been debate in recent years about the relative merits of unilateral nondominant ECT versus bilateral ECT (Lamy et al., 1994; Letemendia et al., 1993; Sackeim et al., 1993). The two techniques probably have equal or near equal efficacy, although unilateral ECT generally requires a longer treatment course, with more treatments being administered. Some patients who are not responding to unilateral ECT will become responders when treatment is converted to bilateral stimulation (Murugesan, 1994). Adverse cognitive effects are probably less severe with nondominant unilateral stimulus application.

Elderly patients, particularly those ravaged by severe melancholic depression, have little metabolic reserve to withstand the passage of weeks waiting for a therapeutic response. "In cases of food refusal it is better to give ECT early rather than wait until the physical state improves, for the contrary is likely to happen" (Gaspar AND Samarasinghe, 1982, p.173). Where ECT is being prescribed because of its superior efficacy and rapid onset of action, we believe it is most appropriate to begin with bilateral stimulation, and revert to unilateral only if undue cognitive complications ensue. As Liang and colleagues (1988) have observed, cognitive function is usually unchanged or improved, even after bilateral ECT treatment.

PHARMACOLOGIC CONSIDERATIONS

Medications are specifically administered in conjunction with ECT with one of two goals: *premedication* to reduce adverse effects of treatment, or *augmentation* of the therapeutic response to ECT.

PREMEDICATION

Eighty percent of ECT complications are cardiovascular in nature (Burke et al., 1985). Hypotension and bradycardia arise from vagal parasympathetic outflow as a direct effect of stimulus administration. Glycopyrrolate is a vagolytic agent that does not cross the blood-brain barrier, and is preferable to atropine, that can produce confusion and delirium (Abrams, 1991). Tachycardia and hypertension ensue with the development of seizure activity in the CNS. Premedication with beta-adrenergic blocking agents can limit these effects. Propranolol, timolol and esmolol all penetrate the blood-brain barrier, and can decrease seizure duration; labetalol does not cross the blood-brain barrier, and does not influence seizure activity (Abrams, 1991).

AUGMENTATION

Because of the high energies required to induce therapeutic seizures in the elderly (Weiner, 1982), patients are often encountered who are showing inadequate seizure response with the maximal output settings on the ECT machine. Seizures may be too brief in duration, or may fail to occur at all. If no agents are identified with the potential for interactions shortening or inhibiting seizure, then administration of pharmacologic agents to modify the seizure response may be necessary. Strategies are available to achieve increased seizure duration or decreased seizure threshold.

Available as an intravenous solution in the United States and as an oral preparation in Canada, caffeine has been used to prolong seizure duration (Kelsey and Grossberg, 1995). We routinely use oral caffeine, 300mg one hour prior to ECT, as a method to lengthen seizures felt to be too short, when stimulus parameters cannot be increased further. The hypothesis that caffeine pre-treatment will allow therapeutic seizures to be attained with lower stimulus energy and commensurate reduction in cognitive side effects remains, to our knowledge, untested.

Failure to obtain generalised seizure activity in the face of adequate stimulus delivery implies the presence of a high *seizure threshold* in the patient. Antipsychotic medications are known to lower the seizure threshold, with some patients maintained on these medications manifesting spontaneous seizures, even in the absence of previous epilepsy (Bezchlibnyk-Butler et al., 1989). This effect is used to benefit in ECT: A dose equivalent to 50 or 100mg of chlorpromazine given one hour prior to treatment may permit a seizure to be obtained with a stimulus that would otherwise prove to be sub-threshold. Low-potency phenothiazines such as chlorpromazine or methotrimeprazine are customarily used, as sedation and anxiolysis prior to treatment is often desirable.

TREATMENT INTERACTIONS

ANAESTHETICS

General anaesthesia for ECT is typically induced with intravenous injection of short-acting barbiturate, methohexital or thiopental. Barbiturates all raise seizure threshold, and phenobarbital continues to be used as an antiepileptic medication. Because of the potential for these agents to reduce seizure activity during ECT, there has been interest in the use of non-barbiturate induction agents. Propafol has been widely studied, but consistent differences have not been found when compared to short-acting barbiturates, in terms either of more rapid recovery from general anaesthesia, or better therapeutic response to ECT (Matters et al., 1995; Kirkby et al., 1995; Malsch et al., 1994; Martensson et al, 1994). The non-barbiturate compound etomidate has been shown to increase seizure duration (Trzepacz et al., 1993; Ilivicky et al., 1995), but it is not routinely available in Canada at present. Dinwiddie and Isenberg (1995) reported that a 45% increase in seizure duration could be obtained with use of a short-acting narcotic together with decreased doses of barbiturate.

ANTICONVULSANTS

Benzodiazepines, frequently used as anxiolytics, sedatives and hypnotics, are also potent anticonvulsants that raise the seizure threshold (Bezchlibnyk-Butler et al., 1989). Benzodiazepine use has been associated with inability to achieve ECT seizure induction, with maximal settings on conventional devices (Lisanby et al., 1996). Alternatively, abrupt withdrawal from long-term benzodiazepine use can precipitate seizures (Ciraulo and Greenblatt, 1996), and the patient administered ECT in the face of rapid benzodiazepine-dose reduction would be at risk for prolonged seizures. Berigan's group (1995) has reported the successful use of the benzodiazepine antagonist flumazenil to temporarily reverse the effects of chronic high-dose benzodiazepine during ECT, without producing prolonged seizures or status epilepticus. Flumazenil has also been used to reverse the effects of benzodiazepines administered to relieve pre-ECT anxiety (Baline et al., 1994).

MAINTENANCE TREATMENT

In his review of the subject, Monroe (1991) advocated recommending ECT as a maintenance therapy for those patients with a recurrent illness that has responded acutely to ECT, and for whom pharmacotherapy alone has failed to prevent relapse or cannot safely be administered. Detailed discussion of outpatient maintenance ECT is beyond the scope of this chapter. However, we will consider maintenance ECT for those with chronic disorders who have benefited from ECT, such as Parkinson's disease or depression in Alzheimer's disease.

SUMMARY

Electroconvulsive therapy is a highly effective treatment for a number of psychiatric and neuropsychiatric conditions. The available data indicates that it can be safely used in the treatment of depression that is comorbid with the common forms of cortical, sub-cortical, and vascular dementias. Side effects associated with ECT tend to be minor and short-term, and there is no evidence whatsoever that the use of ECT hastens the course of dementias. While ECT can produce a characteristic pattern of transient cognitive impairments, when administered to patients with significant dementia at baseline there is no evidence of lasting cognitive deterioration. If standard contemporary procedures are followed, ECT may be safely administered across a wide range of concurrent and comorbid conditions. In many instances, cognitive and behavioural function are improved, presumably because of the amelioration of mood and other non-cognitive symptoms which may be ECT-responsive.

REFERENCES

Abrams R (1991) Electroconvulsive therapy in the medically compromised patient. *Psychiatric Clinics of North America* 14(4):871-885

Atre-Vaidya N, Jampala VC (1988) Electroconvulsive therapy in Parkinsonism with affective disorder. *British Journal of Psychiatry* 152:55-8

Bailine SH. Safferman A. Vital-Herne J. Bernstein S. (1994) Flumazenil reversal of benzodiazepine-induced sedation for a patient with severe pre-ECT anxiety. *Convulsive Therapy.* 10(1):65-8

Benbow SM (1988) ECT for depression in dementia. *British Journal of Psychiatry* 152:859

Bergsholm P, Larsen JL, Rosendahl K ,Holsten F (1989) Electroconvulsive therapy and cerebral computed tomography: a prospective study. *Acta Psychiatrica Scandinavica* 80:566-572

Berigan TR, Harazin J , Williams HL II (1995) Use of flumazenil in conjunction with electroconvulsive therapy. *American Journal of Psychiatry* 152(6):957

Bezchlibnyk-Butler KZ, Jeffries JJ & Martin BA (1989) *Clinical Handbook of Psychotropic Drugs*, 4th Ed. Toronto: Hogrefe & Huber

Burke WJ, Peterson J, and Rubin EH (1988) Electroconvulsive therapy in the treatment of combined depression and Parkinson's disease. *Psychosomatics* 29(3):341-346

Burke WJ Rutherford JL Zorumski CF and Rich T (1985) Electroconvulsive therapy and the elderly. *Comprehensive Psychiatry* 26(5):480-486

Carlyle W, Killick L & Ancill, R (1991) ECT: An effective treatment in the screaming demented patient. *Journal of the American Geriatrics Society* 39:637

Ciraulo DA, Greenblatt DJ, (1996) Sedative-, hypnotic-, or anxiolytic-related disorders, in Kaplan HI & Sadock BJ (Eds.) *Comprehensive Textbook of Psychiatry, 6th Ed. on CD-ROM.* Baltimore: Williams & Wilkins

Coffey CE, Figiel GS, Djang WT, Cress M, Saunders WB & Weiner RD (1988) Leukoencephalopathy in elderly depressed patients referred for ECT. *Biological Psychiatry* 24:143-161

Colp R Jr. (1996) History of Psychiatry, in Kaplan HI & Sadock BJ (Eds.) *Comprehensive Textbook of Psychiatry, 6th Ed. on CD-ROM.* Baltimore: Williams & Wilkins
Dinwiddie SH, Isenberg KE, (1995) Combined alfentanil-methohexital anaesthesia in electroconvulsive therapy. *Convulsive Therapy.* 11(3):170-6

Dubovsky SL, (1986) Using electroconvulsive therapy for patients with neurological disease. *Hospital and Community Psychiatry* 37(8):819-825

Factor SA, Molho ES, Brown DL. (1995a) Combined clozapine and electroconvulsive therapy for the treatment of drug-induced psychosis in Parkinson's disease. *Journal of Neuropsychiatry & Clinical Neurosciences.* 7(3):304-7

Factor SA, Molho ES. Podskalny GD. Brown D. (1995b) Parkinson's disease: drug-induced psychiatric states. *Advances in Neurology.* 65:115-38

Gaspar D, Samarasinghe LA (1982) ECT in psychogeriatric practice—A study of risk factors, indications and outcome. Comprehensive Psychiatry 23(2):170-175

Gottfries C-G (1996) Depression and Alzheimer Disease, in Becker R & Giacobini E (Eds.) *Alzheimer Disease: From Molecular Biology to Therapy.* Boston: Birkhäuser

Hay DP (1996) Electroconvulsive Therapy, in Kaplan HI, Sadock BJ (Eds.) *Comprehensive Textbook of Psychiatry, 6th Ed. on CD-ROM.* Baltimore: Williams & Wilkins

Hurwitz TA, Calne DB, Waterman K (1988) Treatment of dopaminomimetic psychosis in Parkinson's disease with electroconvulsive therapy. *Canadian Journal of Neurological Sciences* 15:32-4

Ilivicky H, Caroff SN & Simone AF (1995) Etomidate during ECT for elderly seizure-resistant patients. *American Journal of Psychiatry* 152(6):957-8

Inglis S, Farnill D (1993) The effects of providing preoperative statistical anaesthetic-risk information. *Anaesthesia & Intensive Care.* 21(6):799-805

Jenike MA (1989) Treatment of affective illness in the elderly with drugs and electroconvulsive therapy. *Journal of Geriatric Psychiatry* 22(1):77-112; discussion 113-120

Kelsey MC, Grossberg GT (1995) Safety and efficacy of caffeine-augmented ECT in elderly depressives: a retrospective study. *Journal of Geriatric Psychiatry and Neurology.* 8(3): 168-172.

Kirkby KC, Beckett WG, Matters RM,. King TE (1995) Comparison of propofol and methohexitone in anaesthesia for ECT: effect on seizure duration and outcome. *Australian & New Zealand Journal of Psychiatry.* 29(2):299-303

Koller WC, Megaffin BB (1994) Parkinson's Disease and Parkinsonism, in Coffey CE and Cummings JL (Eds.) *The American Psychiatric Press Textbook of Geriatric Neuropsychiatry.* Washington, DC: American Psychiatric Press

Lam RW (1990) Treatment of depression in patients with dementia. *American Journal of Psychiatry* 147(1):130-131.

Lamy S, Bergsholm P, d'Elia G (1994) The antidepressant efficacy of high-dose nondominant long-distance parietotemporal and bitemporal electroconvulsive therapy. *Convulsive Therapy* 10(1): 43-52.

Lerer B, Shapira B, Calev A, Tubi N, Drexler H, Kindler S,Lidsky D, Schwartz JE (1995) Antidepressant and cognitive effects of twice- versus three-times-weekly ECT. *American Journal of Psychiatry* 152(4):564-70

Letemendia FJ, Delva NJ, Rodenburg M, Lawson JS, Inglis J, Waldron JJ , Lywood DW (1993) Therapeutic advantage of bifrontal electrode placement in ECT. *Psychological Medicine* 22(2): 349-360.

Liang RA, Lam RW, Ancill RJ (1988) ECT in the treatment of mixed dementia and depression *British Journal of Psychiatry* 152:281-284

Lisanby SH, Devanand DP, Nobler MS, Prudic J, Mullen L, Sackeim HA (1996) Exceptionally high seizure threshold: ECT device limitations *Convulsive Therapy* 12(3):156-64

Lishman, WA (1987) Organic Psychiatry: *The Psychological Consequences of Cerebral Disorder,* 2nd Ed. Boston: Blackwell Scientific Publications

McGuire MH, Rabins PV (1994) Mood Disorders, in Coffey CE, Cummings JL (Eds.) *The American Psychiatric Press Textbook of Geriatric Neuropsychiatry.* Washington, DC: American Psychiatric Press

Malsch E, Gratz I, Mani S, Backup C, Levy S, Allen E, (1994) Efficacy of electroconvulsive therapy after propofol and methohexital anaesthesia. *Convulsive Therapy.* 10(3):212-9

Martensson B, Bartfai A, Hallen B, Hellstrom C, Junthe T, Olander M, (1994) A comparison of propofol and methohexital as anesthetic agents for ECT: effects on seizure duration, therapeutic outcome, and memory. *Biological Psychiatry* 35(3):179-89

Matters RM, Beckett WG, Kirkby KC, King TE, (1995) Recovery after electroconvulsive therapy: comparison of propofol with methohexitone anaesthesia. *British Journal of Anaesthesia* 75(3):297-300

Mendez MF (1996) Neuropsychiatric aspects of epilepsy, in Kaplan HI, Sadock BJ (Eds.) *Comprehensive Textbook of Psychiatry, 6th Ed. on CD-ROM.* Baltimore: Williams & Wilkins.

Moffic HS, Paykel ES. (1975) Depression in medical in-patients. *British Journal of Psychiatry.* 126:346-53.

Monroe RR Jr (1991) Maintenance electroconvulsive therapy. *Psychiatric Clinics of North America* 14(4):947-960

Morley JE (1996) Normal aging: Physiological aspects, in Kaplan HI & Sadock BJ (Eds.) *Comprehensive Textbook of Psychiatry, 6th Ed. on CD-ROM.* Baltimore: Williams & Wilkins.

Murray GB, Shea V, Conn DK (1986) Electroconvulsive therapy for poststroke depression. *Journal of Clinical Psychiatry* 47(5):258-260

Murugesan G (1994) Electrode placement, stimulus dosing and seizure monitoring during ECT. *Australian & New Zealand Journal of Psychiatry.* 28(4): 675-83.

Rasmussen K, Abrams R (1991) Treatment of Parkinson's disease with electroconvulsive therapy. *Psychiatric Clinics of North America* 14(4):925-933

Regestein QR, Murawski BJ, Engle RP (1975) A case of prolonged, reversible dementia associated with abuse of ECT. *Journal of Nervous and Mental Disease* 161(3):200-203

Reichman WE (1996) Neuropsychiatric aspects of cerebrovascular diseases and tumors, in Kaplan HI & Sadock BJ (Eds.) *Comprehensive Textbook of Psychiatry, 6th Ed. on CD-ROM.* Baltimore: Williams & Wilkins

Sackeim HA, Prudic J, Devanand DP, Kiersky JE, Fitzsimons L, Moody BJ, McElhiney MC, Coleman EA, Settembrino JM (1993) Effects of stimulus intensity and electrode placement on the efficacy and cognitive effects of electroconvulsive therapy. *New England Journal of Medicin.* 328(12): 839-846.

Shapira B, Calev A, Lerer, B (1991) Optimal use of electroconvulsive therapy: Choosing a treatment schedule. *Psychiatric Clinics of North America* 14(4):935-946

Small JG, Milstein V, Small IF (1991) Electroconvulsive therapy for mania. *Psychiatric Clinics of North America* 14(4):887-903

Smith LH, Hughes J, Hastings DW, Alpers BJ (1942) Electroshock treatment in the psychoses. *American Journal of Psychiatry* 98:558-61

Snow SS & Wells CE (1981) Case studies in neuropsychiatry: Diagnosis and treatment of coexistent dementia and depression. *Journal of Clinical Psychiatry* 42(11):439-441

Starkenstein SE, Robinson RG (1994) Neuropsychiatric aspects of stroke, in Coffey CE & Cummings JL (Eds.) *The American Psychiatric Press Textbook of Geriatric Neuropsychiatry.* Washington, DC: American Psychiatric Press

Trzepacz PT, Weniger FC, Greenhouse J (1993) Etomidate anaesthesia increases seizure duration during ECT. A retrospective study. *General Hospital Psychiatry.* 15(2):115-20

Tzabar Y. Asbury AJ. Millar K. (1996) Cognitive failures after general anaesthesia for day-case surgery. *British Journal of Anaesthesia* 76(2):194-7

Weiner RD (1982) The role of electroconvulsive therapy in the treatment of depression in the elderly. *Journal of the American Geriatrics Society* 30(11):710-712

Williams-Russo P. Sharrock NE. Mattis S. Szatrowski TP. Charlson ME. (1995) Cognitive effects after epidural vs general anaesthesia in older adults: A randomized trial. *Journal of the American Medical Association* 274(1):44-50

Young RC, Alexopoulos GS, Shamoian CA (1985) Dissociation of motor response from mood and cognition in a Parkinsonian patient treated with ECT. *Biological Psychiatry* 20:566-569

Zwil AS, Pelchat RJ (1994) ECT in the treatment of patients with neurological and somatic disease. *International Journal of Psychiatry in Medicine* 24(1):1-29

9

ENDOGENOUS CORTISOL: RELATIONSHIP TO PSYCHIATRIC DISORDERS

Stephen J. Kiraly, Gergana Dimitrova, and Raymond Ancill

Modern endocrinology traces its roots to the early studies of the effects of steroid hormones on behaviour (Berthold 1849). That research both highlighted the influence of endocrines on behavioural function and opened the door to the study of the relationship endocrine function and psychiatric disorders. During the 1920s, Osler, referring to the mental changes of hypothyroidism noted: "There is striking slowness of thought and movement. The memory becomes defective, the patients grow irritable and suspicious, and there may be headache. In some patients there are delusions and hallucinations, leading to a final condition of dementia" (Osler and McRae, 1924). A short time later, Asher's classic paper on "Myxoedematous Madness", alerted a generation of physicians to the interaction between the brain and the thyroid gland (Asher, 1949). As a result of Asher's work, physicians now routinely screen both young and elderly psychiatric patients for thyroid malfunction. More recently, the introduction of titrated steroid hormones has allowed us to map brain steroid receptors, their pathways and interactions with other neurotransmitter substances. This provides researchers with the tools to examine neuroendocrine function in the context of emergent and chronic psychiatric disorders. One topic, however, that has not been closely studied from a psychiatric perspective is the adrenals and their glucocorticoid effects on brain structures and function. This chapter examines that area with a special emphasis on the implications of adrenal function for the elderly psychiatric patient.

Therapeutics in Geriatric Neuropsychiatry. Edited by R.J. Ancill, S.G. Holliday and A.H. Mithani. © 1997 John Wiley & Sons Ltd

ADRENAL DYSFUNCTION AND PSYCHIATRIC ILLNESS

Cushing was the first to recognize the consequences of adrenal dysfunction noting that hyperadrenalism was associated with "sleeplessness, inability to concentrate, visual disturbances" and "fits of unnatural irritability alternated with periods of depression". Since Cushing's time, there has been considerable progress in understanding the mechanisms through which cortisteroids impact on mental function. Although specific data on the elderly are lacking, the available research suggests that wide fluctuations of or prolonged elevation in glucocorticoid levels are associated with neurotoxicity. Sudden reductions may play a role in inflammatory brain disease and normal levels may prevent stress activated or toxin mediated defense mechanisms from overshooting causing inflammations such as encephalomyelitis (Reder et al., 1994). On the other hand, an excess of circulating glucocorticoids has been noted to be associated with loss of receptors in the hippocampus which is crucial in learning, memory and emotion (Sapolsky, 1992; Young et al., 1995).

It has been noted in the treatment of Cushing's disease that removal of the adrenal glands also improved psychiatric symptoms such as depression (Cohen, 1980). The use of cortisone reverses the mental symptoms of adrenal insufficiency (Addison's disease) even when physical signs are absent (Cleghorn, 1951). Adrenal steroid excess also promotes traits associated with affective disorders such as anxiety, dysphoria, agitation, dyssomnia and psychotic episodes (Dubrovsky, 1993, McEwen, 1987). Medical Letter consultants admonish and cite studies which indicate that exogenous corticosteroids, especially in high doses, can cause mania, depression, paranoia, confusion, hallucinations and catatonia (The Medical Letter Inc. 1993) Normal volunteer non-geriatric subjects are not profoundly affected by small doses of exogenous corticosteroids but 75% reported sadness, restlessness and confusion (Wolkowitz et al. 1990). In laboratory studies, several days of steroid treatment noticeably impaired memory in humans (Newcomer et al. 1994) which itself throws into question recent suggestions that anti-inflammatory drugs might be useful in Alzheimer's Disease.

The overlap between Cushing's syndrome and affective disorder has been well documented in adults (Dubrovsky, 1993; Starkman et al., 1981). Elevated cortisol levels, without the physical stigmata of Cushing's syndrome, have been observed in a number of psychiatric disorders. Depression (Dubrovsky, 1991; Gibbons, 1962, 1964; Nemeroff, 1988; Pearson-Murphy, 1991; Swann et al. 1992), mania (Swann et al., 1992), anxiety (Persky, 1959), dyssomnia (Born et al., 1990), memory and cognitive impairments (Filipini et al., 1991, Wolkowitz et al., 1990) and delusional depressive psychoses (Shatzberg et al., 1985,

Shatzberg et al., 1988) are some examples. Early researchers noted that predisposing factors and vulnerability to depressive illness were correlated with those of Cushing's disease and that mania and depression often preceded the physical signs of Cushing's syndrome (Gifford et al., 1970).

There is also evidence of a significant relationship between stressful life events, cortisol levels, and affective disorders. First, several studies have reported an association between depressive symptoms and stressful, negative life events. (Dohrenwend et al., 1995; Shrout et al., 1989). That relationship, however, is less than perfect and only a small proportion of reported cases of depressions can be accounted for solely by life stressors. Since chronic stress is associated with downregulation and a proliferation of glucocorticoid receptors, one possibility for the occurrence of depression in the context of life-stress is that some people develop an unfortunate cycle of *disorder-event disorder* in which life stressors precipitate adrenal dysfunction which, in turn, precipitates a depressive reaction. This explanation may also help to explain the variable presentations seen in Post Traumatic Stress Disorder (PTSD) and subsets of major depressive illness. It is beyond the scope of this chapter to describe and discuss research findings pertaining to profiles of cortisol levels and DEX resistance in the former syndromes, but it is clear that the HPA axis can play a central role, and that both cortisol levels and DEX sensitivity/resistance are best interpreted in terms of exposure to stress and trauma.

HEURISTIC CASE STUDY

At this point, evidence is presented suggesting that adrenal function may be implicated in the emergence of psychiatric disorders including depression, psychosis and anxiety. In geriatric psychiatry it is common to observe cases of primary affective disorder, often with delusions and agitation, which occur for the first time in old age (Alexopoulos et al., 1988; Gnam et al., 1993, Young et al., 1992). These tend to be challenging cases as the presentations are often atypical, and while there are no clear precipitating events, the symptoms often emerge in the context of significant negative life events. Given the above analysis, it is worthwhile to consider the possibility of adrenal dysfunction as part of the clinical picture. The following case study illustrates a number of the diagnostic and treatment issues involved in managing the elderly client:

> *E.C., an 87 year old woman suffered a number of serious life events, was overwhelmed, depressed and moved to a retirement home where she became increasingly paranoid and agitated. Her primary symptoms included hypomanic behaviour and grandiose delusions, without*

delirium. There was no history of a previous psychiatric disorder. Prior to her decompensation, she had no difficulties with activities of daily living (ADL), coped as a caregiver to a dying husband and was medically stable. At time of first admission, laboratory investigations revealed hyponatremia, hypomagnesemia, and elevated serum cortisol which did not suppress with dexamethasone (DEX). There was some discussion amongst clinicians as to whether she appeared Cushingoid, but consultation with endocrinologists did not yield the diagnosis of Cushing's syndrome. She failed trials of several antidepressant and neuroleptic medications and seized on lithium. Upon hospitalization, electrolyte imbalance was corrected and anticonvulsant medication was instituted. Brief transient improvement was followed by relapse and a second hospitalization during which she was treated with electroconvulsive therapy (ECT). Improvement followed with return of normal sleep pattern and euthymia. Cortisol levels and dexamethasone suppression test (DST) also normalized. CT scan results revealed a small inoperable adrenal adenoma but serum cortisol level was normal and she was asymptomatic. She was discharged to her nursing home, in a much improved condition, without further need for psychotropic medications.

Two questions may be raised on the basis of this interesting presentation regarding the role of adrenal function. First, it is worth asking whether this was a case of subclinical Cushing's syndrome? Second, were HPA axis dysfunction and hypercortisolemia either causal or perpetuating factors in the patient's treatment resistant psychosis?

HPA DYSREGULATION AND PSYCHIATRIC DISORDERS

In answering the above questions, it is important to closely examine the phenomena of hypercortisolemia. The dysregulation of the HPA axis in Cushing's syndrome, depression and psychosis has been a well documented phenomenon (Dubrovsky, 1993). Researchers found that dysregulation in depression differs from dysregulation found in Cushing's syndrome. Normally, cortisol and other steroid hormones are secreted in bursts in a circadian cycle, with highest levels in the morning hours. The normal rhythm architecture is obliterated in the majority of cases in Cushing's syndrome but not in major depression. The hypercortisolism of depression is characterized by higher amplitudes of secretory pulses and higher total cortisol secretion but not an increase in the number of pulses. Sleep disturbance consists of abnormally short rapid eye movement (REM) sleep latencies. In time, antidepressant drugs or

ECT treatments are known to normalize levels of cortisol secretion. In particular, treatment lengthens REM latency, (Pearson-Murphy, 1991; Linkowsky et al., 1987). The age range of the patients in the latter study was from 31-62, leaving room for speculation about the results of a similar study in the geriatric population.

The psychiatric presentation of endogenous hyper-cortisolemia and symptoms of exogenous glucocorticoid administration are dissimilar (Pearson-Murphy, 1991) but cognitive impairments are demonstrable in normal subjects on administration of exogenous corticosteroids (Wolkowitz, Reus et al. 1990, Wolkowitz et al., 1990). Cortisol hypersecretion has been noted to be associated with cognitive impairment when age and depression were studied as independent variables (Rubinow et al., 1984). Further insight into the effects of suppression of serum cortisol may be gained from the response of depressed non-geriatric patients to short term administration of low dose DEX. In preliminary reports and double-blind trials, administration of DEX rapidly improved depression without producing euphoria or other side effects (Arana, 1991). In another sample of seven bipolar patients ranging in age from 18-75 an 85% response rate was found to oral or i.v. DEX administration (Beale et al., 1995). In the latter studies, serum cortisol levels were not reported; therefore, it is not clear how cortisol levels correlated with improvement in mental status. The DST has been proposed as a biological marker for depression but, despite high specificity, it has not proved useful because of low sensitivity (Turner, 1982). Other researchers have found that the hypercortisolemic response to the stress of hypoglycemia was preserved in depression but not in Cushing's syndrome and that this was a reliable discriminatory test between the two conditions (Jeffcoate et al., 1979). In testing for adrenal insufficiency by insulin tolerance test a symptomatic hypoglycemia is necessary to produce an adequate cortisol response (Semenkovich, 1993). This response would be absent in Addison's disease but not in primary affective disorder.

CORTISOL LEVELS AND AGING

It is also important to examine the effects of aging on cortisol regulation. The majority of work in this area has been performed using animal models, although some human experimental results are available. In both rats and primates, the hippocampus loses neurons with age. There is a gradual hippocampal corticosteroid receptor loss resulting in decreasing feedback inhibition and age related increasing serum cortisol levels (Coleman et al., 1987, Landfield, 1994; Sapolsky, 1992). It has been well established that adrenalectomized rats do not show the "normal" hippocampal cell loss that is associated with aging (Landfield et al; 1994).

In the case of the human hippocampus, the situation is similar to the extent that there is age related neuronal loss. However, basal serum cortisol levels do not rise proportionately with age, not at least to about age 75. After age 75, elderly humans tend to be both hypercortisolemic and DST resistant (Sapolsky, 1992, Greden et al., 1986). This pattern stands in contrast to that observed in the rat which shows a steady age related decline. The suggestion that the aged hippocampus does not suffer dysfunction is most likely an artifact caused by an overrepresentation of people under the age of 75 (the "young" elderly) in the study samples.

In humans, the maintenance of normal function in the under 75 age groups appears to be maintained by two complementary processes. First, there is an age related decline in glucocorticoid production. Second, there is an age-related decline in clearance and excretion. The combined effect of these processes is a longer half-life in the blood stream and lower urinary corticosteroid concentrations (Sapolsky, 1992). It should also noted that even in the young elderly there are some subtle defects which appear to be similar to what has been found in aging rats and baboons. For example, when challenged with doses (0.5mg DEX) that are lower than the standard (1.0 mg DEX), the healthy aged are DEX resistant at a higher rate than are their younger counterparts. In other words, even the healthy aged tend to be borderline feedback resistant and thus potentially susceptible to hypersecretion of cortisol.

Additionally, there are diseases which are common in old age such as Dementia of the Alzheimer's type (DAT), which are associated with HPA dysregulation and hypercortisolemia independently of basal age related changes (Sapolsky, 1992). Patients with DAT (and depressives) have higher rates (50%) of hypercortisolemia and DEX resistance (APA Task Force, 1987) than matched controls.

ST. VINCENT'S HOSPITAL GERIATRIC PSYCHIATRY RESEARCH UNIT CORTISOL STUDY

The case of E.C., taken in the context of the general issues that have been highlighted in the above brief review, prompted us to further study the nature of hypercortisolemia in the elderly. The documented effects of hypercortisolemia on cognitive and limbic functions, the known prevalence of hypercortisolemic states in acute psychiatric hospital admissions (50%), and high rate of treatment resistance amongst psychotic geriatric patients, suggested to us that we should begin by examining cortisol levels in geriatric psychiatry inpatients. We anticipated that if we could find a systematic relationship between cortisol levels and psychiatric status it could serve to help identify groups of patients that would exhibit preventable side effects of chronic or intermittent elevated cortisol levels, including memory loss and osteoporosis. To test this expectation we formulated a general hypothesis that "fasting, morning cortisol levels would correlate with the demographic and psychiatric profiles patients". The specific factors to be tested in the light of this hypotheses were *age, psychiatric diagnosis, presence of treatment resistance,* and *gender.*

Methodology: Fifty-three consecutive admissions to a psychogeriatric inpatient clinic were screened for inclusion in the study. Of these 53, 6 were excluded leaving a group of 47 study participants. The age and sex distribution of subjects is presented in Table 1.

Table 1. Age and Sex of Participants

Age Range	62 - 90
Median Age	77
Old (62-74)	16 (34%)
Old-Old (75-84)	24 (51%)
Oldest-Old (85-90)	17 (15%)
Males	15 (32%)
Females	32 (68%)

As may be seen in Table 1, 32 (68%) of subjects were female and 15(32%) were male. The sample was also stratified into three age levels representing the old, the very old, and the extremely old. This allowed for the data to be examined adjusting for the observed difference in cortisol regulation between the old and the very old. The majority of subjects (65%) were over the age of 74.

Fasting AM cortisol levels were obtained for all subjects. Cortisol levels were reported in nmoles/L (nM) with a cutoff at 550 nM (550 nM = 20 ug/dl). (This value turned out to be slightly lower than the mean value obtained in the study).

This was also consistent with the adjusted normal value given by Goodman & Gilman and the levels established by Linkowski (1951). The values were then grouped into two categories: NORMAL (< 550 nM), and HIGH (>550 nM). The descriptive statistics for cortisol level are presented in Table 2.

Table 2. Cortisol Levels for Study Subjects

	nM
Range	190 - 1026
Mean	561
Median	524
SD	192

As may be seen in Table 2, the mean cortisol level for the sample was 561 with a median of 524 and a range of 190 to 1026.

The first analysis examined the relationship between age and cortisol levels. The distribution of the dichotomized (normal, vs. abnormal) data across the three age groups was examined. Those data are presented in Table 3.

Table 3. Cortisol Values by Age Group*

	NORMAL (<550 nM)	HIGH (>550 nM)
Old (n=16)	10 (21.3%)	6 (12.8%)
Old-Old (n=24)	12 (25.5%)	12(25.5%)
Oldest-Old (n=7)	12 (98%)	1(2.1%)

* statistically not significant

As may be seen in Table 3, the old-old (age 75-84) had the greatest incidence of high values (25.5%) followed by the old (12.8%) and the oldest-old (2.1%). The overall difference in the distribution of values, however, was not statistically significant.

The second analysis focused on the psychiatric diagnosis of the patients. Subjects were divided into two groups: *DEPRESSION*, which included all affective disorders with or without psychosis and dementia and *DEMENTIA* which included all cases of dementia without affective disorder or paranoid psychosis. This dichotomy accounted for 43 of the 47 subjects. Six subjects with neither depression nor dementia were excluded from the analysis. The distribution of diagnoses and cortisol values is presented in Table 4.

Table 4. Cortisol Values by Diagnosis*

	NORMAL (<550 nM)	HIGH (>550 nM)
DEMENTIA (n=21)	14(67%)	7(33%)
DEPRESSION (n=22)	11(50%)	11(50%)

*not statistically significant

As may be seen in Table 4, there was a slightly greater occurrence of high values (50% vs. 33%) in the groups with depression, but the difference was not statistically significant. The results, however are consistent with earlier reports that up to 50% of acute psychiatric admissions present with elevated cortisol levels.

The third analysis examined the relationship between cortisol levels and treatment resistance. For this study, treatment resistance was defined as failing three or more trials of treatment with either neuroleptics, antidepressants or ECT. Using this criterion, 20 subjects were classified as treatment resistant. The distribution of cortisol levels across over the two groups was then examined.

Table 5. Treatment Resistance by Cortisol Level *

	NORMAL (<550 nM)	HIGH (>550 nM)
NON-RESISTANT (n=27)	16(59%)	11(41%)
RESISTANT (n=20)	12(60%)	8(40%)

* Not statistically significant

As may be seen in Table 5, there was little difference between diagnostic category and cortisol levels. For both groups, approximately 40% exhibited high cortisol levels.

The final analysis focused on gender. The data were grouped by sex (male, female) and the distribution of cortisol levels was then examined.

Table 6. Gender by Cortisol Level *

	NORMAL (<550 nM)	HIGH (>550 nM)
MALES (n=15)	13(87%)	2(13%)
FEMALES (n=32)	15(47%)	17(53%)

*significant, p <.001

As may be seen in Table 6, there was a marked difference in the distribution across gender categories with a much larger percentage (53% vs 13%) of the females exhibiting high cortisol levels. This difference was highly significant (p<.001).

DISCUSSION

These results indicate that the null hypothesis was rejected in the case of gender differences in cortisol levels. For the other analyses, age, diagnostic categories and treatment resistance were not shown to be significantly related to elevated cortisol levels. The significant finding that elderly females tend to have higher cortisol levels than to males has clinical implications. Cognitive impairment, dementia, mood disorders and osteoporosis are all more prevalent in females, especially elderly females with psychiatric illness. If chronic or recurrent elevations in cortisol levels are etiological, then it behooves us to try antiglucocorticoid strategies to reduce this risk factor.

It should be recognized that this was a relatively small, open case-series study and is subject to the limitations of such non-experimental designs. There are several other methodological issues that may be of importance in the design of future research in this area. The first, and most important, is the issue of cortisol measurement. Because cortisol is rapidly secreted with a very short half-life, the timing of measurements is critical. Instead of fasting, AM levels, it may be useful, particularly in symptomatic cases, to collect bedtime measures. Alternately, 24 hour urine levels yield accurate data, although they are hard to collect.

The second issue relates to the potential for an age effect. Although the data in this study did not demonstrate a significant effect for age, the 75-84 age group demonstrated the greatest incidence of high cortisol values. Until further studies settle the issue one way or another, it seems prudent to look carefully for age effects and to stratify study samples age.

Despite the fact that cortisol levels did not reliably differentiate between groups, the fact remains that a significant number of these elderly, difficult to treat patients had high cortisol values. Since high cortisol levels are associated with mental and behavioural problems, irrespective of psychiatric status, it is important to consider both the diagnostic and treatment implications of cortisol dysfunction.

DIAGNOSTIC AND TREATMENT ISSUES

Antiglucocorticoids. It is known that dexamethasone can be acutely used to reduce circulating cortisol levels with notable beneficial effects on mood and irritability (Arana, Beale). It is also known that long term administration does not keep cortisol levels down and DEX itself has peripheral glucocorticoid effects. True Cushing's syndrome has been successfully treated with cortisol antagonists such as ketoconazole, metyrapone and glutethimide (Angeli et al. 1985; Feldman, 1986; Sonino, 1987; Sonino et al., 1986). The rationale of using specific *antiglucocorticoids* in the treatment of major depression was reviewed recently and the preliminary results of a small study were reported. In that study, four patients with chronic, severe, treatment resistant depression were treated with the glucocorticoid antagonist mifepristone (RU486) for up to eight weeks with reduction in the mean scores on the Hamilton Rating Scale for Depression observed for three patients (Pearson-Murphy et al., 1993).

Furthermore, a review of the literature on hypercortisolemia as a factor in maintaining affective psychosis, revealed cases of treatment resistant affective psychosis, with or without Cushing's disease, that positively responded to cortisol antagonist therapy (Jeffcoate et al., 1979; Kramlinger et al., 1985; Ravaris et al; 1988) Also. in an open clinical trial of major clinical depression in the absence of Cushing's syndrome, ten patients, all under age 65, were given two month's treatment with steroid suppressant drugs and no specific psychiatric treatment. Six of the 10 demonstrated marked improvement that was maintained for over five months after withdrawing the drugs. Side effects were mild to moderate. The authors concluded that, "The results provide some evidence that steroids are involved in the maintenance of depression, and that their suppression may lead to a readjustment of the hypothalamic-pituitary-adrenal axis with remission of depression." They also pointed out that treatment resistant patients form an important proportion (up to 28%) of the depressed population; therefore, it was important to note this rather dramatic response. In the same sample, after recovery, some patients reported "being able to think more clearly" (Pearson-Murphy et al., 1991).

More recently, in a case report of a 4-week, double-blind trial followed by a 14 week period of open label treatment of a refractory depression with an antiglucocorticoid, Anand reported a considerable reduction of depressive symptoms (Anand et al., 1995). Thakore also reports that in an open series of eight patients who met the DSM-III-R criteria for major depression, cortisol synthesis inhibition normalized serotonergic subsensitivity while reducing ambient cortisol levels. In that study five patients recovered from their depression while the rest improved. The authors concluded that lowering serum cortisol was a safe and effective method of treating a subset of depressions and urged double blind studies (Thakore et al., 1995). These findings are consistent with previous experimental observations that corticosteroid receptors are down-regulated in the brain with chronic stress (Dallman,1991). Up-regulation of brain cortisol receptors may be important as a possible treatment intervention.

Pharmacological Options. A number of glucocorticoid antagonists have been used by researchers and clinicians to produce effects ranging from adrenal tissue destruction (chemical adrenalectomy) to specific intracerebral glucocorticoid receptor blockade. Neurons containing corticosteroid-specific receptors are located in the hippocampus, septum and amygdala. These areas are involved with memory, mood and behaviour. Given that other steroids play a prominent role in behaviour, it is not surprising that some pathophysiologists believe that adrenal steroids have a more direct relationship to major depressive illness.

Mitotane, a compound similar to DDT (o,p'-DDD), has been used to selectively destroy the adrenal medulla in Cushing's syndrome. This is an alternative to surgical adrenalectomy. Clearly, it has no place in the treatment of psychiatric syndromes but it is important to note that psychiatric symptoms associated with Cushing's syndrome cleared rapidly after its administration (Starkman et al., 1986).

Available antiglucocorticoids are presented in Table 7.

Table 7. Antiglucocorticoids

Inhibition of cortisol biosynthesis:	**metyrapone** **aminoglutethimide** **ketoconazole**
Glucocorticoid receptor blockade:	**mifepristone (RU486)**
ACTH inhibition:	**ketoconazole** **cyproheptadine**

Each of the above listed medications can cause significant side effects. As a means of dealing with this problem, they are often used in combination at lower dosages than would be the case if they were used singly. In using these drugs, it is also important to note that therapeutic effects are transient because the HPA axis compensates for the reduction in circulating cortisol. Mifepristone (RU486) is itself a steroid and a blocker of glucocorticoid and progesterone receptors. It also has side effects and is rarely given to humans for more than a few days. Cyproheptadine is an antiserotonergic which inhibits ACTH secretion. Bromcriptine and valproate have also been tried with inadequate results. The clinician should also be aware that there are few data on the use of these compounds with elderly patients.

There is some evidence that adaptive coping responses can modulate the HPA axis response to exposure to stress. The availability of behavioural outlets, efforts at affective or behavioural coping or control over a stressful stimulus/environment is known to reduce HPA axis responses in rodents, primates and humans (Breier et al., 1987; Dallman, 1991; Gunnar, 1992; Voigt et al., 1990, Weiss, 1968; Weinberg et al., 1980). This has implications for residents of long term care facilities and their caregivers. As Sapolsky remarked, "I can imagine few settings that better reveal the nature of psychological stress than a nursing home" (Sapolsky, 1994). The use of relaxation and breathing exercises, mild physical exercise, regularization of sleep patterns, and control of levels of stimulation in the environment are ways of managing environmental stressors.

CONCLUSIONS

Hypercortisolemia disrupts sleep, energy level, mood and cognition. It is probable that the vulnerable, aged brain is susceptible to the dangers of elevated endogenous cortisol levels in much the same fashion as to exogenous steroidal anti-inflammatory drugs. Theoretically, by blocking cortisol biosynthesis and more specifically, by producing cortisol receptor blockade in the hippocampus, the psychotic enabling effects of hypercortisolemia may be mitigated or prevented. Although research data on hormonal actions on brain steroid receptors in the aging population are sparse, there is some experimental evidence and clinical opinion pertaining to the younger adult population that rapid response can be obtained in a subset of depressions, with or without psychosis, by correcting HPA axis over-activity. Given that a number of relatively safe glucocorticoid antagonists are available, well controlled, follow-up studies of glucocorticoid inhibition in the treatment of psychiatric syndromes accompanied by hypercortisolemia are indicated.

In geriatric psychiatry, where low tolerance of standard treatment methods such as psychotropic drugs and ECT are often problematic and where treatment resistance is not uncommon, selected cases may well respond to antiglucocorticoid therapy. Some preliminary trials in this are would break new ground without sacrificing safety.

REFERENCES

Alexopoulos GS, Young RC, Meyers BS (1988) Late onset depression. *Psychiatr Clin North Am*, 2:101-115

Anand A, Malison R, McDougle CJ, Price L.H. (1995) Antiglucocorticoid treatment of refractory depression with ketoconazole: a case report, *Biol. Psychiatry* 37:338-340

Angeli A, Frairia R (1985) Ketoconazole therapy in Cushing's disease, *Lancet* 1:821.

APA Task Force on Laboratory Tests in Psychiatry (1987) The dexamethasone suppression test. An overview of its current status in psychiatry", *Am J Psychiatry* 144:1253-1268

Arana GW (1991) Dexamethasone for the treatment of depression: a preliminary report, *J Clin Psychiatry* 52(7):304-306

Arana GW (1991) Intravenous dexamethasone for symptoms of major depressive disorder, *Am J Psychiatr*, 148(10):1401-1402

Arana GW, Santos AB, Laraia MT, McLeod-Bryant S, Beale MD, Rames L.J. (1995) Dexamethasone for the treatment of depression; a randomized, placebo-controlled, double-blind trial, *Am J Psychiatry* 152(2):265-267

Asher R (1949) Myxoedematous madness, *British Medical Journal* 2:555-562.

Beale MD, Arana GW (1995) Dexamethasone treatment of major depression in patients with bipolar disorder, *Am J Psychiatry* 152(6):959-960

Berthold AA (1849) Transplantation der Hoden Arch Anat Physiol Wiss Med, 16:42-46

Born J, de Kloet ER, Wenz H, Kern W, and Fehm HL (1991) Gluco- and antiminaralocorticoid effects on human sleep: a role for central corticosteroid receptors, *Am J Physiol* 260:E183-E188

Breier , Albus M, Pickar D, Zahn TP, Wolkowitz OM, Paul SM Controllable and uncontrollable stress in humans: alterations in mood and neuroendocrine and psychophysiological function, *Am J Psychiatry* 1987;144:1419-1425

Cleghorn RA (1951) Adrenal cortical insufficiency: psychological and neurological observations, *Canad M A J* 65:449-454

Cohen S (1980) Cushing's syndrome: a psychiatric study of 29 patients, *Brit J Psych* 136:120-124

Coleman P, and Flood D (1987) Neuron numbers and dendritic extent in normal aging and Alzheimer's disease, Neurobiol Aging, 8:521-540

Cushing H (1913) Psychiatric disturbances associated with disorders of ductless glands, *Am J Insanity,* 69:965-990

Cushing H (1935) Basophil adenomas of the pituitary body and their clinical manifestations *Bull John Hopkins Hstl*, 50:137-195

Dallman MF (1991) Regulation of adrenocortical function following stress In: Brown MR, Koob GF, River C, eds Stress: neurobiology and neuroendocrinology New York: Marcel Dekker, p 173-192

Dohrenwend PB, Shrout PE, Link BG, et al (1995) Life Events and Other Possible Psychosocial Risk Factors for Episides of Schizophrenia and Major Depression: A Case-Control Study, in Does Stress Cause Psychiatric Illness?, Edited by Mazure CM, Washington, DC, American Psychiatric Press Inc, pp 43-65

Dubrovsky B (1991) Adrenal steroids and the physiopathology of a subset of depressive disorders, *Med Hypotheses,* 36:300-305

Dubrovsky B (1993) Effects of adrenal cortex hormones on limbic structures: Some experimental and clinical correlations related to depression, *J Psychiatr Neurosci* 18(1):4-16

Feldman D (1986) Ketoconazole and other imidazole derivatives as inhibitors of steroidogenesis, *Endocr Rev,* 7:409-420

Filipini D, Gijsbers K, Birmingham MK, Kraulis I, Dubrovsky B (1991) Modulation by adrenal steroids of limbic function, *J Steroid Biochem Molec Biol,* 39(2):245-252

Gibbons JL (1962) Plasma cortisol in depressive illness, *J Psychiat Res* 1:162-171

Gibbons JL (1964) Cortisol secretion rate in depressive illness, *Arch Gen Psychiatry* 10:572-575

Gifford S, Gunderson JG (1970) Cushing's disease as a psychosomatic disorder: a selective review of the clinical and experimental literature and a report of ten cases, *Persp Biol Med,* Winter:169-221

Gnam W, and Flint AJ (1993) New onset rapid cycling bipolar disorder in an 87 year old woman, *Ann J Psychiatry,* 38:324-326

Greden J, Flegel P, and Haskett R (1986) Age effects in serial hypothalamic-adrenal-pituitary monitoring, *Psychoneuroendocrinology,* 11:195-203

Gunnar MR (1992) Reactivity of the hypothalamic-pituitary-adrenocortical system to stressors in normal infants and children, *Pediatrics,* 90(Sept suppl):491-497

Jeffcoate WJ, Silverstone JT, Edwards CRW, and Besser GM (1979) Psychiatric manifestations of Cushing's syndrome: response to lowering of plasma cortisol, *Q J Med,*48:465-472

Kramlinger KG, Peterson GC, Watson PK, and Leonard LL (1985) Metyrapone for depression and delirium secondary to Cushing's syndrome, 26:67-71

Landfield PW Nathan Shock Memorial Lecture 1990 The role of glucocorticoids in brain aging and Alzheimer's disease: an integrative physiological hypothesis (Review) Experimental Gerontology 1994;29(1):3-11

Landfield PW, and Eldridge JC (1994) Evolving aspects of the glucocorticoid hypothesis of brain aging; hormonal modulation of neuronal calcium homeostasis (Review), *Neurobiology of Aging,* (4):579-88

Linkowsky P, Mendleewicz J, Kerkhofs M, LeClercq R, Golstein J, Brasseur M et al (1987) 24-hour profile of adrenocorticotropin, cortisol and growth hormone in major depressive illness: effect of antidepressant treatment, *J Clin Endocrinol Metab* 65:141-148

McEwen BS (1987) Glucocorticoid-biogenic amine interactions in relation to mood and behaviour, *Biochem Pharmacol,* 36(11):1755-1763

Medical Letter Inc (The), (1993) 35(901):65-70

Murphy BEP, and Wolkowitz OM (1993) The pathophysiologic significance of hyperadrenocorticism: Antiglucocorticoid strategies, *Psychiatric Annals,* 23(12):682-690

Nemeroff CB (1988) The role of corticotropin-releasing factor in the pathogenesis of major depression, *Pharmacopsychiat,* 21:76-82

Newcomer JW, Craft S, Hershey T, Askins K, and Bardgett ME (1994) Glucocorticoid induced impairment of declarative memory performance in adult humans, *J Neurosci,* 14:2047

Osler W and McRae T (1924) The Principles and Practice of Medicine, 9th edition, D Appleton & Co, New York, 1924, p 867

Pearson-Murphy BE (1991) Steroids and depression, *J Steroid Biochem Molec Biol* 38(5):537-559

Pearson-Murphy BE, Dhar V, Ghadirian AM, Chouinard G, and Keller R (1991) Response to steroid suppression in major depression resistant to antidepressant therapy, *J Clin Psychopharmacol,* 11(2):121-126

Pearson-Murphy BE, Filipini D, and Ghadirian AM (1993) Possible use of glucocorticoid receptor antagonists in the treatment of major depression: preliminary results using RU 486, *J Psychiatr Neurosci,* 18:209-213

Persky H (1959) Blood corticotropin and adrenal weight-maintenance factor levels of anxious patients and normal subjects, *Psychosom Med,* 21:379-386

Ravaris CL, Sateia MJ, Beroza KW, Noordsy DL, and Brinck-Johnsen T (1988) Effect of Ketoconazole on a hypophysectomized, hypercortisolemic, psychotically depressed woman, *Arch Gen Psychiatry,* 45:966-967

Reder AT, Thapar M, and Jensen MA (1994) A reduction in serum glucocorticoids provokes experimental allergic encephalomyelitis: implications for treatment of inflammatory brain disease, *Neurology,* 44(12):2289-94

Rubinow DR, Post RM, Savard R, Gold PW (1984) Cortisol hypersecretion and cognitive impairment in depression, *Arch Gen Psychiatry,* 41:279-283

Sapolsky RM (1992) How does a Neuron Die? Stress, the aging brain and the mechanism of neuron death, MIT, Boston Part II, p 119-258

Sapolsky RM (1992) In Stress, the aging brain and the mechanism of neuron death MIT, Boston, Ch 14, p 315-317

Sapolsky RM (1994) Why zebras don't get ulcers, W H Freeman and Company, New York, p 268

Schatzberg AF, Rothschild AJ, Langlais PJ, Bird ED, and Cole JO (1985) A corticosteroid/dopamine hypothesis for psychotic depression and related states, *J Psychiat Res,* 19(1):57-64

Schatzberg AF, and Rothschild AJ (1988) The roles of glucocorticoid and dopaminergic systems in delusional (psychotic) depression, *Ann NY Acad Sci*, 537:462-471

Semenkovich CF (1993) Endocrine diseases In: Woodley M, Whelan A, eds Manual Medical Therapeutics Boston: Little, Brown & Company

Shrout PE, Link BG, Dohrenwend BP, et al (1989) Characterizing life events as risk factors for depression: the role of fateful loss events, *J Abnorm Psychol* 98:460-467, 1989

Sonino N The use of ketoconazole as an inhibitor of steroid production N Engl J Med 1987;317:812-818

Sonino N, Boscaro M, Fava GA, and Mantero F (1986) Prolonged treatment of Cushing's disease with metyrapone and glutethimide, *IRCS Med Sci,* 14:485-486

Starkman MN, and Schteingart DE (1981) Neuropsychiatric manifestations of patients with Cushing's syndrome Relationship to cortisol and adreno-corticotrophic hormone levels, *Arch Intern Med,* 191:215-219

Starkman NM, Schteingart DE, and Schork MA (1986) Cushing's syndrome after treatment: changes in cortisol and ACTH levels and amelioration of the depressive syndrome, *Psychiatr Res,* 19:177-188

Swann AC, Stokes PE, Casper R, Secunda SK, Bowden CL, Berman N, et al (1992) Hypothalamic-pituitary-adrenocortical function in mixed and pure mania" *Acta Psychiatr Scand,* 85:270-274

Thakore JH, and Dinan TG (1995) Cortisol synthesis inhibition: a new treatment strategy for the clinical and endocrine manifestations of depression, *Biol Psychiatry* 37:364-368

Turner WJ (1982) Dexamethasone suppression test: problems and promise (editorial) *Biol Psychiatry,* 17:1-2

Voigt K, Ziegler M, Grunert-Fuchs M, Bickel U, and Fehm-Wolfsdorf G Hormonal responses to exhausting physical exercise: the role of predictability and controllability of the situation, *Psychoneuroendocrinology,* 15:173-184

Weinberg J, and Levine S (1980) Psychobiology of coping in animals: the effects of predictability, In: Levine S, Ursin H eds Coping and Health New York: Plenum: 39-59

Weiss JM (1968) The effects of coping on stress, *J Comp Physiol Psychol,* 65:251-260

Wolkowitz OM, Reus VI, Weingartner H, Thompson K, Breier A, Doran A et al (1990) Cognitive effects of corticosteroids, *Am J Psychiatry,* 147(10):1297-1303

Wolkowitz OM, Rubinow D, Doran AR, Breier A, Berrettini WH, Kling MA et al (1990) Prednisone effects on neurochemistry and behaviour, *Arch Gen Psych* 47:963-968

Young EA, Kwak SP, and Kottak J (1995) Negative feedback regulation following administration of chronic exogenous corticosterone, *J Neuroendocrinol* 7(1): 37-45

Young RC, and Klerman GL (1992) Mania in late life: focus on age at onset, *Am J Psychiatry* 49(7):867-876)

10

DEMENTIA: THE NURSE'S ROLE

Lorraine Lyons and Catherine Schindell

Nursing has long had a role in the care and support of the person with dementia. As we move toward the millennium, the nursing role in the area of geriatric psychiatry is becoming ever broader and more important. Nursing services today are provided to the geriatric population in a variety of settings including general hospitals and specialized units, psychiatric long-term care facilities, outpatient mental health clinics, adult day programs, and the person's own home. The responsibilities of the nurse include not only the provision of basic care but the additional challenges of working in partnership with medical specialists and multi-disciplinary teams to identify and treat various types of dementia. In addition, the nurse meets problems such as depression, psychosis, aggression, agitation, and disinhibited behaviour that emerge in the course of dementing illnesses.

The nurse who cares for the geriatric psychiatry population is challenged to combine psychiatric nursing knowledge with an understanding of the normal aging process, physiological disorders, and socio-cultural factors which influence the elderly and their families (Baldwin et al., 1995). In particular, nurses working in the community or providing discharge and follow-up services to community facilities must master a wide range of skills including:

- assessing coping skills and resources of the caregivers
- counseling and educating caregivers

Therapeutics in Geriatric Neuropsychiatry. Edited by R.J. Ancill, S.G. Holliday and A.H. Mithani. © 1997 John Wiley & Sons Ltd

- directing nursing interventions toward both patient and caregivers
- collaborating with other members of the professional health care team
- coordinating with other institutions, community agencies, and support organizations

Until recently, once a diagnosis of dementia was established, there was little to offer in the way of treatment, cure or hope. Individuals went home to face the slow but steady decline they knew was inevitable. When the disease had progressed to a point where their care needs became too complex to be met by dedicated family and community support workers, they were placed in care facilities.

That situation is slowly and irrevocably changing. The introduction of new dementia treatment compounds (see Chapters 2 and 9) provides a means for challenging the course of what have been thought to be incurable diseases. The advances being made in the use of traditional compounds to treat the psychiatric disorders and dysfunctional behaviours provide more effective medical management of problems that historically required isolation or close observation. In addition, nursing practice has become much more sophisticated in terms of managing the behaviour of persons with dementia. Together, these advances make it possible to more effectively treat and manage the geriatric patient with dementia.

Today, nurses providing care to persons with dementia are challenged to provide excellent assessment and knowledge of current treatment and management strategies to meet the multiple needs. Providing and coordinating nursing care to these patients can be complex. The geriatric psychiatry nurse as a primary care provider must be thorough in assessing cognitive, affective, functional, physical, and behavioural status. The global, multi-area losses exhibited by persons with dementia, the complications of physical illness, and the need to establish a safe and secure environment for the patient demand this type of multi-dimensional approach.

BEHAVIOURAL RESPONSES

Within Geriatric Psychiatry, "behavioural problems" are often a symptom of underlying pathology. The nurse must learn to differentiate between behaviours that are symptoms of treatable conditions, and behaviours that are non-medically related. The first step in assessing a behaviour is to precisely describe it. Once it is clear what is to be monitored, the nurse can record its frequency, duration, and any precipitating factors. A comprehensive behavioural assessment is important both as a basis for planning nursing care and as a basis of accurate communication with an attending physician.

Since behavioural changes are often the early signs of physical and mental disorders, the emergence of dysfunctional behaviour is most properly viewed as an indicator of an underlying cause.

Among the frequently identified "problem behaviours" are:

- **aggressiveness** - may present as irritability, destructiveness or violence toward self and/or others; verbal or physical response to internal or external precipitants; impaired impulse control.

- **agitation** - may present as restlessness, noisiness, pacing with no apparent purpose, psychomotor expression of emotional tension, anxiety, fear, over-stimulation or stress.

- **apathy** - the absence or suppression of emotions or feelings; an indifference to what is generally stimulating and of interest.

- **emotional changes** - may be irritable, may present with saddened or labile mood and blunted affect.

- **illusions** - misinterpretation of environmental/external stimuli.

- **indecisiveness** - as the disease progresses the individual may have increasing difficulty making decisions.

- **repetitive actions** - the involuntary and pathological persistence of an idea, action or response.

- **psychotic symptoms** - hallucinations (usually auditory or visual perception that do not result from an external stimulus); delusions (false fixed beliefs). "One should specifically inquire about the most common delusions - harm, infidelity, and theft." (Dian, 1996).

It is also important to identify *who* is concerned by the behaviour - the patient, the family, peers, or unrelated caregivers and *why* the behaviour is a concern.

Caregiver response to behaviour must be assessed because it may reinforce or increase disturbed behaviour. The patients and their families may also be anxious and distressed by behavioural changes.

FUNCTIONAL ABILITIES

As the dementia progresses, patients become less aware of their deficits and their resulting limitations.

> *As cognitive function deteriorates over a period of years, most Alzheimer's patients become progressively less aware of the extent, or even the existence, of their deficits. Recent evidence indicates that this diminishing of awareness in Alzheimer's patients is accompanied by an increase in confabulations on memory tests and by a decline in frontal lobe function* (Schachter, 1996).

Each member of the health care team plays a vital role in the assessment of functional abilities. However, in some settings major assessment and coordination is the responsibility of the nurse. The nurse's assessment of the patient's functional abilities includes the following:

- **mobility** - aspects to be assessed include the patient's ability to move safely within the environment, participate in necessary activities, and maintain contact with others. A thorough nursing assessment of the risk for falls is also necessary to ensure a safe environment.

- **activities of daily living (ADLs)** - activities of daily living such as bathing, dressing, eating, grooming, and toileting are concrete and task-oriented. They provide an opportunity for purposeful nurse-patient interaction. It is important to encourage patients to be as independent as possible in performing their own ADLs.

- **physiological functioning** - assessment of physical health is especially important with the demented patient because of the interaction of multiple chronic conditions, the presence of cognitive deficits, and the frequent behavioural presentation of physical health problems.

- **nutrition** - the dementia patient may need assistance to ensure adequate nutrition. As well as the normal problems of aging, the patient with dementia frequently has additional coordination and swallowing problems.

  The nurse must routinely evaluate the patient's dietary needs. Unmet nutritional needs may potentiate such problems as skin breakdown, inadequate absorption of medications, and impaired wound healing.

- **medications** - the nurse administers, monitors, documents and communicates observations regarding the effects of the prescribed medications (Salzman, 1992) (Luke, 1990). New medications now available to the patient with dementia require enhanced nursing knowledge concerning their administration, side effects and desired results. Further, the nurse will be responsible to promote the education of caregivers and provide support and education to the caregivers.

NURSING ASSESSMENT PROCEDURES

> *A vast majority of older adults have no cognitive impairment, but for those who do, an accurate assessment is essential to ensure that treatable conditions are not overlooked* (Miller, 1990).

Assessing the geriatric psychiatry patient's health and functional status is a complex process. Because of the great diversity of symptoms and numerous atypical presentations, the assessment of illness in geriatric clients often requires a detective-like or puzzle-solving approach, rather than the usual diagnostic process (Miller, 1990).

Assessment includes not only identifying dementia-related mental and behavioural changes but also evaluating present and potential factors which may threaten health. It is also the basis for planning, intervening, and evaluating nursing care uniquely aimed at maintaining and optimizing the patient's state of health. A careful nursing assessment also supports the decisions and interventions of the health care team. And, when properly conducted, it can provide the basis for ongoing and systematic evaluation of treatment efficacy.

A variety of specialized assessment tools and procedures have been developed to provide a means of objectively evaluating the areas that are critical to the care of persons with dementia. The ones most commonly used in our geriatric psychiatry inpatient program are listed below in Table 1.

TABLE 1
NURSING ASSESSMENT TOOLS

Nursing assessment tools used to monitor behaviour and assess for effectiveness of treatment are as follows:

- ❑ Nursing database

- ❑ Scale for Nursing Assessment in Geriatric Psychiatry (Geri-SNAP)

- ❑ Scale for Aggressive Behavioural Responses in the Elderly (SABRE)

- ❑ Sleep Chart

- ❑ Food and Fluid Intake Record

- ❑ Movement Chart

- ❑ Weight Chart

- ❑ Agitation Chart

- ❑ Patient/Resident Care Plan

- ❑ Medication Administration Record

The *Nursing Database* contains basic demographic, social, medical, and other relevant information. It is updated as needed.

The *Geri-SNAP* was developed to highlight types of dysfunction that are commonly seen in geriatric psychiatric disorders. It includes both functional and psychiatric variables and is designed to be used sequentially on a weekly basis to provide a longitudinal picture of patient status.

The *SABRE* is a structured tool for identifying and quantifying aggressive behaviour in geriatric patients. It allows the nurse to identify specific types of aggressive behaviour and to differentiate among different types of aggression. It was designed to be used on a weekly basis, but can be adapted to either shorter or longer time-frames.

The *Sleep Chart* is a generic means of recording the sleep patterns of geriatric patients. Our version involves half-hourly checks of the patients with indication of whether the patient is asleep. It may be filled out nightly if there is a suspicion of a sleep disturbance or periodically as a monitoring procedure.

Food and Fluid Forms are often critical to the care of geriatric patients. Regardless of the particular recording format, these charts must contain precise measurements of caloric and fluid intake. This is especially important in diagnosing depression as well as establishing the presence of illness. Similarly, the *Weight Chart* is an important record and may be completed on a regime that is dictated by the condition and needs of the patient.

The *Movement Chart* was developed at St. Vincent's Hospital to help monitor the treatment of Parkinson's disease in geriatric patients. It permits the nurse to monitor specific movement problems including cogwheeling and initiation difficulties. It is particularly useful in helping to establish efficacy levels and dosing patterns in patients being treated for Parkinson's disease. It is also useful in monitoring parkinsonism in patients treated with neuroleptics.

Agitation Charts are used to document the type and frequency of agitated behaviour (see chapter 5 for a detailed presentation of agitation), while the *Medication Administration Record* provides the basic information on the pharmacological treatment of the patient.

THE ASSESSMENT OF CO-MORBID ILLNESS: DEPRESSION AND DELIRIUM

Delirium and depression are among the more common causes
of acute and subacute deterioration in patients with dementia.
(Ancill, 1993).

Because treatable comorbid conditions such as depression or delirium may present with behaviours similar to those of dementia, it is essential to differentiate among these conditions.

Depression occurs frequently in patients with dementia. Since the patient with dementia may have an impaired ability to communicate symptoms, the nurse must be skilled in detecting behavioural changes associated with the depression. The use of nursing assessment tools such as the sleep chart, the SABRE aggression chart, and the Geri-SNAP assist the nurse to identify and quantify these behaviours. Included when assessing for depression in the patient who has dementia are (Ancill, 1993):

- Dysphoria, fatigue or anergia
- Fitful sleep with frequent distressed wakenings
- Nonspecific dysfunctional behaviour such as agitation, importuning, aggression, pacing, yelling
- Suicidal behaviour
- Diurnal variation of dysfunctional behaviour
- Nonspecific psychotic symptoms such as paranoia

Patients with dementia are also at great risk of developing delirium. Physicians or nurses never recognize approximately 70% of patients who become delirious as being in a delirious state (Foreman, 1991). The nurse must therefore be vigilant in observing for symptoms of delirium:

- Disorientation, often fluctuating
- Transient memory loss
- Night/day reversal
- Hallucinations
- Illusions
- Agitation and fearfulness
- Delusions

A complete investigation may be needed following any abrupt behavioural change as it may have an underlying physical cause, such as dehydration, infection, or medication reaction. The most common differential diagnostic issue is whether the person has a dementia rather than a delirium, has a delirium alone, or has a delirium superimposed on a pre-existing dementia. The nurse's clear understanding of the symptoms of each of these conditions promotes the provision of specific data needed for an accurate diagnosis.

MANAGING THE PATIENT WITH DEMENTIA – SOME BASIC POINTS

Caring for the patient with dementia is a complex task. Because patients with dementia are often disoriented, have receptive and expressive language deficits, exhibit both recent and remote memory loss, and present with behavioural disturbances, providing even basic care can be difficult. The patient may not understand what the nurse is trying to do, may perceive the nurse as aggressive or frightening, and may be unable to effectively inhibit an inappropriate response. With patience and care, however, the nurse can not only provide effective services to the demented patient, but also help the person to adjust to care-giving routines.

The basic principles of interacting with patients with dementia are few and simple. Always treat the person with respect. The nurse should consciously work to avoid patronizing the patient. Establish rapport with the patient. Persons with dementia respond, as do all people, to expressions of care and concern, albeit sometimes in limited ways. Finally, keep in mind, treatment follows from assessment. The nurse working with the demented patient should always be aware of the patient's basic medical and nursing profile. Being alert to changes from baseline levels of function will often give the nurse a head-start in identifying and managing problems.

Some of the common management situations encountered in geriatric psychiatry settings, together with the specific skills that the nurse can bring to the situation, are presented below.

Disorientation: Persons with dementia invariably exhibit some degree of disorientation. When coupled with memory loss, this can leave the patient thoroughly confused about the temporal and physical environment. This can lead to difficult situations as, for example, when the confused and disoriented person tries to leave the facility to return "home."

Several techniques work well with confused, disoriented patients. First, one-to-one communication works far better than having several people approach and talk to the patient. It is often effective to nominate one person to communicate with the patient, even if two or more nurses may be involved in the procedure. This makes it easier for the patient to remain engaged, rather than having to constantly shift attention when different people talk - a task that is particularly difficult for patients with dementia.

Second, it is important to establish contact with the person, and to understand whatever it is that they may be trying to communicate. It is counterproductive to confront the patient, even if their beliefs are clearly false. Reality orientation and related procedures seldom prove useful. It is generally more effective to use positive focus comments to reassure and settle the person. For example, if an 80-year-old patient says, "I have to pick up my daughter from school" a positive, affirming comment such as "You sound like a very concerned mother" may have a calming effect. This technique, when used with gentle redirection, such as saying, "I was talking with your daughter this morning and she said she will visit you after work today," often works well.

Because the confusion and disorientation seen in dementia are seldom remediable, there is little benefit in challenging beliefs and perceptions. Calm reassurance will ordinarily be a much more effective approach than any other technique.

Providing Physical Care: Common problems encountered with the provision of physical care to the demented patient often concerns personal care, bathing and toileting. This is not surprising, as these areas involve a variety of potentially sensitive issues including personal modesty, fear, miscomprehension, pain and discomfort.

In dealing with physical care issues, various techniques are useful. Approaching the patient from the front and moving slowly provides the person with opportunity to apprehend and adjust to a care-giver's presence. A simple explanation of what is happening establishes contact and reassures the patient. Repetition is a very useful technique and can be particularly helpful when the person has severe memory impairment. Moving in a step-by-step fashion and taking as much time as is possible to help the person feel comfortable minimizes agitation in the patient. Recognition of the individuals need for privacy should be a feature of the care plan, and particularly so with reference to bathing and changing clothing.

Concerning the patient with a history of poorly controlled aggression occuring in the context of providing personal care, timing care-giving procedures with the administration of either regular or PRN medication may be helpful. The judicious use of medication can, if fact, make the care-giving process much easier to bear for the patient and improve safety for the staff.

Agitation: It is important to recognize that agitation has a physical cause and requires medical treatment. Despite this caveat, there are certain basic management techniques that can help to control agitation or prevent it from escalating. The first step is to provide an appropriate physical environment. It is well established that excess stimulation or an unstructured environment precipitate or exacerbate agitated behaviour. Rapidly changing environments are also associated with the emergence of agitated behaviour. Nurses should be aware of this and pay particular attention to the person prone to agitation.

If a person begins to exhibit agitation, the *early* administration of a PRN medication can often stop the escalation. The timing of the PRN is important, as it is easier to intervene at the beginning of an episode than later in the sequence.

If PRN medication is not an option, one to one care can often be effectively used to control the agitation. The nurse working with the agitated patient can use such a technique as actively slowing the pace of interaction by talking slower, walking slower, etc. The nurse can also use re-direction and distraction to defocus the person from this pattern of behaviour. Supportive communication appears to be the best technique with patients who are disoriented.

Aggressiveness. Aggressiveness in the demented patient is one of the most difficult behaviours to manage. As the patient with dementia is frequently incapable of expressing concerns, nursing staff may initially find it very difficult to determine the cause of aggression. The nurse must rely on observational skills to complete the most thorough assessment possible. Quantifying aggression has proven difficult as the term is quite subjective and everyone's interpretation of and tolerance toward aggression is different.

To ensure interventions are evaluated accurately, a timely and efficient mechanism to capture the number of aggressive episodes is helpful. Since its interpretation is so subjective, clearly definable categories are needed. A scale which could be used by the nurse to record any type of aggressive episode displayed in a 24-hour period is SABRE. This tool allows the nurse to record the type of aggression observed, and note whether it was spontaneous or in response to a stimulus. Once the number and type of episodes are captured, it is easier to evaluate whether or not an intervention is having the desired effect on the behaviour.

Medication Administration: Nurses must ensure that patients take their prescribed medications. This is not as simple as it sounds, as elderly patients, and particularly those who are frail or confused, may be unwilling or unable to accept their medication. Since oral ingestion is the most common method used with persons with dementia this will be the focus of discussion.

It is essential that the nurse be aware of any swallowing impairment the patient may have. If such is the case the nurse might initiate a referral to a speech language pathologist/occupational therapy for a swallowing assessment. Gelled or thickened fluids might alleviate minor problems. It may be that a different preparation or method of administration of the medication might be more appropriate for a particular patient. Since many demented patients resist pills, the nurse should always be looking for new alternatives to disguise taste, texture, etc. Applesauce, ice-cream, honey, jam, pudding, pureed fruit and gelled juices are all substances that might make medication more palatable and easier to swallow. The patient's dietary preferences or religious restrictions must be considered when choosing among the options.

If there is suspicion that a person is spitting out or hiding medication, the nurse should carefully observe the person during and immediately after medication.

The nurse also has an obligation to carefully monitor and then document any observed side effects. Since the person with dementia may not be able to clearly identify side effects, the nurse must be aware of the common problems associated with the patient's medication and regularly check to see if such effects are emerging.

SUMMARY

Accurate, comprehensive, and organized data collection is one of the most crucial responsibilities of the nurse, and especially so concerning the demented patient. As demented patients may not recognize problems they are experiencing with their health, or they may not be able to communicate these problems, it is essential to have on-going observation of patient responses, so that changes can be identified early and their significance evaluated by the team.

There are a number of other areas which require close monitoring and clear documentation including agitation and aggression, food and fluid intake, elimination, sleep, self care, mood and affect, suicidal ideation, orientation and level of consciousness.

Documentation is vital for effective communication with the health care team. It is a necessary function for the assessment, planning, implementation, and evaluation of the patient's care.

Increasingly, research is providing us with new understanding, new knowledge and new insights to assist us in better treating and caring for the demented patient and giving the patient, the family, and the nurse, reason for hope.

REFERENCES

Ancill RJ (1993) Depression and dementia: Assessment and Treatment. *Geriatrics,* 27-34

Baldwin BA, Stevens GL, Friedman SD (1995) Geriatric psychiatric nursing. In Stuart GW, Sundeen SJ (eds.) *Principles and Practice of Psychiatric Nursing*, St. Louis: C.V. Mosby Co

Dian L (1996) Diagnosis and Treatment of Dementia. *The Canadian Journal of CME*, February: 135-142

Foreman M (1991) The cognitive and behavioural nature of acute confusional states *Scholarly Inquiry for Nursing Practice,* 5(1): 3-16

Luke EA Jr (1990) Psychotropic drugs. In Hogstel, M.O. (ed) *Geropsychiatric Nursing*, St. Louis: C.V. Mosby Co

Miller CA (1990) Nursing care of older adults: theory and practice. London: Scott, Foresman/Little Brown Higher Education

Salzman C (1992) Clinical geriatric psychopharmacology (2nd Ed.) Baltimore: Williams & Wilkins

Schacter DL (1996) Searching for memory. BasicBooks: New York

11

PSYCHOTHERAPY WITH THE GERIATRIC PSYCHIATRY PATIENT

Cheryl E. Henry and Paul E. Sungaila

This chapter will discuss psychotherapeutic interventions with the geriatric psychiatry patient. We will examine several key elements of psychotherapy with this unique patient group. In addition, this chapter looks at how the dynamics of challenging comorbid illnesses can complicate the therapeutic process. Throughout this chapter we do not distinguish between the terms counseling and psychotherapy. Despite distinctions which have been made, our contention is that an effective therapeutic approach will encompass, where appropriate, change in the patient's psychic function in some fundamental way; and/or support and education of their existing social system. We shall take the perspective that the patient's experience of symptoms always takes place in a social context which shapes the experience. And that the onset of symptoms almost always results in changes in the patient's role in his or her social group, be it family, work group, or care facility.

BASICS OF INTERVENTION

The fundamental principles of psychotherapy are paramount in any therapeutic relationship, regardless of the patient's age. Carl Rogers developed a "client-centered" approach which held that psychological growth would occur if patients were provided with the "necessary and sufficient conditions" of empathy, respect and unconditional positive regard. This basic but essential therapeutic attitude, in combination with a theory based approach, excellent

Therapeutics in Geriatric Neuropsychiatry. Edited by R.J. Ancill, S.G. Holliday and A.H. Mithani. © 1997 John Wiley & Sons Ltd

communication skills and a sound knowledge of self, will guide the therapist in all interventions. Even the most seasoned therapist, however, must add to their repertoire a sound knowledge of issues which are relevant to specific aged patients. The following areas are seen as key to therapy with the geriatric psychiatry population.

Firstly, a basic knowledge of gerontology will enhance the therapist's appreciation of many issues pertaining to the elderly patient. This will include the ability to differentiate normal from abnormal aspects of aging related to health and social function (Novak, 1995). In addition, a basis in gerontology will allow the therapist to move beyond societal myths regarding the aging process, culminating in a therapeutic relationship based on facts instead of misperceptions.

Also essential in the therapeutic process is an assessment which results in the therapists' full appreciation of the patient in the context of his/her generation, personal history and social system. The therapist must focus on understanding the patient's *subjective experience*. If the patient perceives the therapist as not understanding their experience, both past and present, the opportunity for the patient and therapist to form a therapeutic alliance may be lost (Knight, 1986). While modern medicine is based on objective observation and scientific method, to practice *the art of healing*, understanding the patient's subjective experience is critical. Only in the context of taking a full history can the therapist appreciate the patient's experience and acknowledge decades of both positive and negative life events.

And finally, the psychogeriatric patient will likely be affected by one or more comorbid illnesses. In psychiatry, patients communicate symptoms through verbal description and nonverbal behaviour. Symptoms are often experienced as pervasive, vague and difficult to describe. These experiences may include feelings of distress and beliefs which the patient may well know are irrational or demeaning. The therapists' knowledge of the impact of the illness(es), which overlay the normal course of aging and premorbid function, is integral to the therapeutic process. For therapists whose background is not in psychiatry or medicine, updates on the onset and course of specific illnesses, such as depression or Alzheimer's disease, will prove essential in working with the dynamics of this patient population (Knight, 1986).

THE GERIATRIC AGED PATIENT–MYTHS VS REALITY

The geriatric patient, by virtue of age, is a member of a very large and diverse societal group. *Aging and Canada* estimates that by the year 2000 the elderly, those individuals aged 65 years and older, will comprise 13% of the population in developed nations such as the US and Canada (Novak, 1995). Many myths and social stereotypes exist about the elderly. In beginning work with this patient group the therapist will need to be aware of society's attitudes and beliefs. Areas such as physical capability, mental and sexual function and lack of adaptability are some examples of where myth and misperception prevail. The therapist can look to the field of gerontology, the study of aging, to provide a welcome balance of information which measures fact against myth.

Gerontological research focuses on many societal issues pertaining to the elderly. It looks at demographics as well as the very real problems of poverty and social isolation amongst the aging population. Gerontology also explores sources of myth, and thereby creates an appreciation of the pervasive nature of society's misperceptions. As Novak points out in *Aging and Canada* (1995), one source of prejudice against older people is the media. He notes newspaper stories sometimes blame the elderly for rising health care costs. In addition, greeting cards are noted as an unfailing source of 'humour' and sarcasm which focus on the pitfalls of old age. On a more positive note, however, Novak (1995) notes that very little media attention is focused on the fact that the majority of elderly retire in good health and carry on with satisfying lives. They often take up new careers, schooling or volunteer work. This is possible because, contrary to popular myth, learning continues into old age. According to Aging and Society (1995), while the older adult may take a somewhat longer time to learn new skills, intellectual function does not decrease as a matter of course with aging. And of course, contrary to popular belief, sexual function and intimacy can remain a vital part of life well into old age.

The vast majority of older adults remain independent, requiring little or no assistance to engage in the activities of normal living. This belies the myth that large numbers of the elderly live in institutions. As Novak (1995) reports, the reality is that institutionalization increases with age. Only 3.3 % of 65-74 year olds live in nursing facilities. And on a another hopeful note, in contrast to myths depicting consistent misery in old age, a 1988 Health and Welfare Canada (Novak, 1995) survey indicates that only 30 % of seniors reported life as being very or fairly stressful (compared to 52 % of those 55 or younger).

Society's false beliefs regarding the elderly would appear to be well entrenched. The therapist will be challenged to develop an understanding of the geriatric psychiatry patient in the context of this overall prejudice. But, no doubt, both the therapist and the patient will benefit from an approach which is based on fact and not false assumptions. With a broad, factual perspective as its base the therapeutic relationship can proceed with its objective of maximum therapeutic gain.

THE THERAPIST'S OPPORTUNITY FOR SELF EXPLORATION

Working with the elderly patient can be a deeply satisfying experience. The patient, by virtue of age, offers the therapist the opportunity to explore issues of both a personal and historic nature.

On a personal level, the therapist is directly challenged to review his/her own beliefs. First and foremost, the therapist must ascertain if his/her own attitude about aging is based on factual information or general societal myth. A non-factual belief system may determine the willingness to even proceed with an elderly patient. Working with a patient whom, because of age, the therapist automatically views as inherently miserable or unable to learn new skills, will, undoubtedly, have an impact on the therapeutic relationship.

In addition, the therapist may be challenged to more fully appreciate his/her own thoughts pertaining to aging, death and relationships with older adults in their own family of origin. The therapist who has explored personal issues will be less likely to encounter problems with counter transference.

Countertransference, as defined by Knight (1986), refers to either the therapist or client bringing into the therapeutic relationship responses learned from previous experiences. Very often these responses were learned in the context of family. When a patient responds to the therapist in a manner which denotes pre-existing unresolved issues, the response should become a part of the therapy. However, as Knight aptly notes, if the therapist responds to the patient as if they were a family member..."it is less appropriate because it is, after all, the client's therapy" (p.132).

While it is beyond the scope of this chapter to provide an indepth section on countertransference issues, readers are encouraged to review works by Knight (1986) and Levine (1996). It would seem apparent that by virtue of age the geriatric patient is capable of evoking issues of which the therapist was previously unaware. In order that the therapeutic relationship not be clouded by issues which are the therapist's, self exploration, perhaps assisted, may be required.

PERSON BEFORE PATIENT–THE IMPORTANCE OF PERSONAL HISTORY AND SOCIAL ENVIRONMENT

The geriatric patient suffering from Alzheimer's disease or other psychiatric and co-morbid illness will frequently present with a miriad of symptoms which can obscure pre-morbid function and personality. For all involved, it is relatively easy for the symptoms to become the primary focus. Subsequently, the perspective that the illness is an overlay to the *underlying person and personal history* may not receive adequate emphasis.

A thorough assessment is one which will explore current stressors, personality and coping strategies, social supports and pre-morbid function. The therapist's understanding of the patient in the context of their personal history is fundamental to the 'client centered' relationship and to all subsequent therapeutic gains. The relating and documentation of the history can be a rich and rewarding experience for both parties. In it the patient's subjective experience is honored and the therapist hears the gift of history. In addition, both the therapist and patient may glean valuable insight into the role which the past plays in current behaviours.

AN APPRECIATION OF GENERATIONAL VALUES

The study of the patient in the context of personal history can easily begin with an exploration of the commonly held values and practices of that era. Values and beliefs, at both a personal and societal level, are powerful driving forces in any generation. Subsequently, the therapist must understand the values and beliefs of the patient's generation in order to appreciate decisions which the patient has made or will make (Knight, 1986). Forearmed with knowledge, or at least a willingness to explore these powerful forces, the therapist will be less likely to engage in attempts to change the patient's thinking. Rather, the process will be one of exploring available options given the patient's decision on any given topic.

Elderly patients report significant societal change over their life time. Values pertaining to marriage, family and work, for example, may appear to the older adult to bear little resemblance between the past and present. While the elderly patient may indeed have difficulty relating to societal change, the younger therapist may, without reflection, attempt to work with the patient in the context of current values.

The womens movement, for example, has resulted in significant societal change for both sexes. As is aptly noted by Levine, (1996) the concepts of freedom of choice and self-determination have become integral to the modern woman. In the generation of the elderly patient, however, such was not the case. The therapist must subsequently be cautious to not view the patient's lifestyle or decision making as unhealthy. What may appear as dependence, for example, is merely a reflection of the parameters of that generation. When the standards of the generation are kept in perspective, the elderly woman who never drove, wrote a cheque or worked outside the home can be appreciated in an entirely different context. Expectations regarding marital harmony, as noted by Levine (1996) is another area where the therapist is quite likely to encounter significant differences in behaviour between the generations. It has not been the norm for the older generations to divorce. But instead of judging past behaviours from the perspective of current times, Levine (1996) suggests that the older generation has much to teach... "about the values they embraced which supported their ability to form and maintain relationships over a long and often difficult span of time". An open and inquisitive stance will afford the therapist the opportunity for many rich learning experiences.

Maintaining a perspective of the patient in the context of history acts as a counter to myth as well as an explanation of behaviour. The myth of the older generation's rigidity and resistance to change can easily be countered when one considers the multiple losses inherent with age. The elderly patient has, for example, adapted to war(s), seen the loss of siblings, friends, possibly spouse and ultimately health. Even in the face of the older generation's under representation as a client group in therapy (Levine (1996), this is understandable in the context of the generation. As Knight (1986) notes the older generation have had less exposure to, or informal education, about psychotherapy and outpatient services. "Throughout much of their lives, mental health meant long term stays for psychotic individuals in locked wards in state hospitals far from home". For the elderly patient and therapist whose therapeutic encounter is as a result of ill health and not choice, the experience will be ultimately more rewarding for both when built on a framework of historical appreciation.

PERSONAL HISTORY

Once the framework of a historic or generational perspective has been established, the therapist's next step is to elicit the patient's personal story within that context. The optimum scenario is for the patient to tell his/her own story. However, if that ability is impaired by illness, the therapist must look to the next best person, likely a family member, to assist the patient. To hear the story is not only a necessary part of the therapeutic process, it is also a privilege. The therapist is given the opportunity to envision the patient's premorbid function and inherent capabilities and as well is provided with valuable information which can be incorporated into the therapy. It is important to note that in situations where the patient is unable to provide their own history the family often welcome the opportunity.

A thorough personal history will be one which explores major events and milestones throughout the patient's life. Beginning with the family of origin the therapist will elicit data on birth place, family constellation and relationships. It will be important to track the history of illness, losses and family communication style. Exploring family of origin issues is a powerful and informative part of the therapeutic process. Regardless of the patient's age he/she remains emotionally connected to the family system and as such must be considered an individual functioning within that context (Sieburg, 1985). It is widely believed, for example, that the loss of the mother in the patient's early childhood can set the stage for later life depression (Beach, 1990). And while other family members may never be physically present in any therapy session, their impact will be noted. What the patient took away from family, including the previous generations, will have been incorporated throughout a lifetime of relationships and decision making (Papero, 1990).

Other areas which the therapist should consider for inclusion in the personal history are education, employment, hobbies, social function, war experience, trauma, culture, spirituality and, of course, marital history. Any or all of the above mentioned categories will provide valuable clues to past coping style and can easily be indicators of unresolved issues which can be discussed in the therapy.

THE SOCIAL SYSTEM

Understanding the patient in the context of their social system is another essential component of the therapeutic process. No one, regardless of age, goes about their lives without influencing or being influenced by their emotional and physical environment. Whenever possible the therapist must incorporate and include those persons integral to the patient's life. How the family, for example, understands the patient's illness and views his/her experience with therapy may either enhance or diminish therapeutic gain. Marital relations is one area which must be explored in depth as it... "holds, at a minimum, considerable influence over feelings of well-being" (Beach, 1990, p.53). In considering treatment for depression, it is noted by Beach that the marital situation may often play a central role in the development and continuation of the illness. Concomitantly, bereavement, and the patient's perception of the loss must be thoroughly explored. While bereavement is, as noted in Beach (1990), a universal human condition, the death of a spouse is a very traumatic experience. *In Suicide and*

Depression in Late, Life one of several studies referenced on elderly suicide, found that 21% who committed suicide had reported bereavement within 6 months prior to the suicide (Plutchik, 1996).

In instances where the patient is a resident of a care facility, the therapist must consider the staff as part of the patient's social system and review the impact of institutional living with the patient. Within the confines of confidentiality, the therapist must ensure that the staff are aware of the patient's therapy. From a systems perspective, family members and facility staff can be included and educated to appreciate the dynamic of their involvement in the situation. Valuable insights may be gained and subsequent behavioural changes may occur. In reviewing the patient's social system the therapist also needs to be aware of the broader social issues which affect the elderly. Sadly, social isolation and poverty are a reality for many elderly. As is cited by Novak (1995), Health and Welfare Canada (1988a) found that approximately one third of unattached older adults (those living alone or in a household not comprised of family members) lived in poverty, most of these were women. While the therapist may have no capacity to effect practical change, the ability to empathize will be enhanced with knowledge. The therapist should also be aware of community resources in order to facilitate additional referrals.

To exclude the patient's social system from the therapeutic process is to ensure that everyone, including the patient, the therapist and important others are operating in a vacuum where optimum therapeutic gain will not be achieved.

PSYCHIATRIC ILLNESS AND THE GERIATRIC PATIENT

A thorough assessment of the patient will have provided the therapist with an understanding of the patient's stressors, social supports (or lack thereof), personality and coping style, plus current and premorbid function. Subsequently, the therapist will be better able to appreciate the impact of the illness on the individual. While it not the responsibility of the non-medical therapist to diagnose specific illnesses, any therapist involved with this patient group must be able to identify and appreciate the dynamics of the illnesses specific to geriatric psychiatry. Commonly, although not exclusively, the older psychiatric patient will experience symptoms of depression, Alzheimer's disease and other forms of cognitive impairment. Often these are seen in conjunction with comorbid physical illness.

An effective therapeutic outcome can be expected only when the therapist knows the patient, recognizes the symptoms and is familiar with the onset and course of an illness. The therapist is then able to intervene with a strategy designed to fit the specifics of the situation. A therapist who is familiar with the various illnesses is aware, for example, that features of cognitive impairment are common to both depression and Alzheimer's disease. That therapist also knows that the treatment approaches are quite different given the etiology of the illnesses. While the Alzheimer's patient will benefit from therapy in the early stages of the illness, cognitive therapy as treatment for the depressive symptoms will, for example, become counterproductive as the cognitive decline continues. As the disease process continues the therapist may intervene primarily with the family of the patient and offer assistance as they cope with illness and loss of the Alzheimer's patient (Kennedy, 1996). With the depressed patient, however, the therapist can begin using cognitive therapy and carry through with that approach matching pace and intensity to the resolution of symptoms and personality of the patient. The use of Reality Orientation as an intervention will vary with the therapist knowledge of the progression of Alzheimer's disease. As Jones (1995) notes, "The central aim is to reorientate people back into reality, although whose reality remains a contentious ethical concern's". One questions the sense of constantly reminding a patient that they are wrong when they are unable to retain the corrections and simply do not believe the new information anyway.

TYPES OF THERAPY

The types of therapeutic intervention must, as previously stressed, follow a thorough assessment of the patient and match the type and stage of the symptom presentation. The following section is offered as examples of various theories and approaches.

Empathy is the key to the psychotherapeutic attitude. Also essential to this attitude is a clear communication between the therapist and patient about concrete behaviour. It is generally useless to talk in abstract generalities. It is much more useful to talk about specific instances. This applies to both diagnostic and treatment interviews. Rather than:

> **Therapist:** do you get anxious often?
> **Patient:** yes all the time

try –

Therapist: tell me about the last time you were anxious. Form a picture in your mind of that situation...where did it occur? when? who was there?

In treatment interviews, one should avoid general discussions about problems, and move towards specific images. For example, if a patient is discussing a longstanding pattern of interpersonal rejection, rather than discussing "your longstanding troubles with people", the therapist might more usefully ask the patient to describe a specific instance of rejection, what the patient thought and felt at the time, what the consequences were, and so on.

ALZHEIMER'S DISEASE

Alzheimer's disease is experienced by patients as a frightening, puzzling, complex of events. In the early stages, patients are often aware of their lapses in cognition. Patients with the disease have anxiety or depressive features. These can be treated with standard anxiety management techniques including progressive relaxation, imagery, and cognitive restructuring.

As the disease progresses, simplification of daily routines and reassurance are the key. Specific guidelines for the management of cognitively impaired persons have been presented (see e.g. D. Williams, 1987). Avoid unnecessary decisions (don't ask if he'd like lunch now, rather, state, 'it's time for lunch'). Family involvement is important to maintain consistent support for the patient. This may require individual therapy for the primary caregiver. The patient's spouse, for example, may wish to explore life-stage issues in his/her own life, or changes in their role as the patient's disorder progresses. The patient's children will need to cope with their own feelings of loss, guilt, or helplessness.

DEPRESSION

Depression is the forum within which cognitive behavioural therapies were developed by Aaron Beck (Beck, Rush, Shaw, and Emery, 1979) and others, including Ellis, Mahoney, and Meichenbaum. The cognitive-behavioural therapies focus on the patient's beliefs about the world and how these beliefs generate maladaptive patterns of emotion and behaviour. Any combination of losses in earlier life may lead to lifelong assumptions such as "I'm always on the verge of failure". Such a person might devalue their achievements, creating idious circles of self-defeating behaviour and rejection. Since aging is associated with numerous losses, such a person might develop a major depressive episode in response to triggers such as retirement, death or disability of a spouse or close friends, or financial stress.

Cognitive-behavioural therapy uses an active, directive, structured approach to problem solving specific target symptoms. For a detailed presentation of the treatment see Beck and Young (1985) and Fennell (1989). The typical protocol involves 10-20 one hour weekly or twice weekly sessions focusing on identifying assumptions and beliefs underlying maladaptive behavioural patterns. The first few sessions are devoted to the assessment of longstanding problems, associated negative thoughts, the current events triggering the depressive syndrome, and current thoughts of poor self esteem or hopelessness. A treatment rationale is then developed which is based on behavioural recording of specific negative episodes and the patient's resulting thoughts and feelings. This is followed by a weekly review of these episodes and consequences, followed by specific interventions such as challenging false assumptions, and altering the patient's daily routings to maximize rewarding experiences. Reminiscence groups and life review have also been demonstrated as effective with the elderly depressed patient (Burnside, 1994)

CONCLUSION

In conclusion, psychotherapy with the geriatric psychiatry patient appears to be a viable, yet underutilized intervention. It is well documented that the emotional and psychlogical problems of the elderly are undertreated (Soukup, 1996; JAMA, 1992) and often lead to needless disability and caregiver burden. It also appears to be well documented, although perhaps not widely sought information, that the elderly population is quite capable of benefitting from psychotherapeutic intervention. It is hoped that the therapist who is perhaps interested in working with this patient group will be prompted to focus their interests and specialties and pursue work within this rich and rewarding field.

REFERENCES

Beck AT, Rush AJ, Shaw BF, Emery G (1979) *Cognitive Therapy of Depression, NY: Guilford Press*

Beck AT and Young, JE (1985) Depression. In DH Barlow (ed) *Clinical Handbook of Psychological Disorders* NY: Guilford Press: 206-244

Burnside I (1994) Reminiscence and life review: therapeutic interventions for older people, *Nurse Practioner* (4) 55-61

Beach SR (1990) Depression and Marriage, *NY: Guilford Press*

Fennell MJV (1989) Depression" In Hawton K, Salkovskis PM, Kirk J, Clark (eds). *Cognitive Behavior Therapy for Psychiatric Problems* NY: Oxford: 169-234

Jones A (1995) How effective is reality orientation for elderly, confused patients? *British Journal of Nursing 4*, (9) 519-525

Kennedy GJ (1996) The epidemiology of late-life Depression in Suicide and Depression. In *Suicide and Depression in Late Life, NY: J Wiley*

Knight B (1986) *Psychotherapy with Older Adults*, Newbury Park: Sage Publications

Levine L (1996) "things were different Then": Countertransference issues for younger female therapists working with older female clients", *Social Work in Health Care, 22(4)* 73-88

Novak MW (1995) "Aging and Canada", Scarborough: Nelson Canada

NIH Consensus Development Panel on Depression in Late Life (1992) Diagnosis and treatment of depression in late life, *JAMA* 268(8); 1018-1023

Papero DV (1990) Bowen family systems theory. *Boston: Allyn and Bacon*

Plutchik R (1996) Clinical measurement of suicidality and coping in late life". In *Suicide and Depression in Late Life* Kennedy G(ed) NY: JWiley

Seiburg E (1985) Family Communication, An Integrated Systems Approach, NY: Gardner Press

12

THE COGNITIZATION OF DEMENTIA

S.G. Holliday, R.J. Ancill and L. Myronuk

DEMENTIA: A progressive organic mental disorder characterized by chronic personality disintegration, confusion, disorientation, stupor, deterioration of intellectual capacities, and impairment in the control of memory, judgement, and impulses (Mosby's Medical Dictionary).

A BRIEF HISTORICAL PERSPECTIVE

Historically, the term dementia has referenced a loss of the power of the mind. Mind, in this context, was traditionally taken to mean more than mental ability and incorporated what we now think of as judgement, moral behaviour, and personality. To be demented meant to become less than human, as it involved loss of all that was thought to make humans unique. Dementia is referenced in the Bible, the works of Shakespeare, and in many other historical literary and medical texts, always in the sense briefly described above.

Medical thought on the characteristics of dementia has more or less paralleled the common language conception. Even today, a common medical definition of dementia (see above) focuses on the occurrence of deterioration in a number of areas that are thought to be expressions of brain function - personality, cognition, impulse control, and so on.   In the normal process of medical advances, broad descriptive terms, such as dementia, eventually give way to more precise descriptors of the specific diseases that produce common symptoms. Modern medicine has, in fact, recognized several types of dementia. In the early 20th century the term *senile dementia* was used to describe loss of function that occurs in the senium. *Dementia praecox* was also introduced by

Therapeutics in Geriatric Neuropsychiatry. Edited by R.J. Ancill, S.G. Holliday and A.H. Mithani. © 1997 John Wiley & Sons Ltd

Emil Kraepelin to describe a general loss of function that occurs early in life (Kraepelin, 1909). While dementia praecox evolved into the neuropsychiatric disease known as schizophrenia, senile dementia exhibited a different course. The descriptor senile was gradually removed from diagnostic systems, largely because the constellation of symptoms that mark dementia in the elderly were also occasionally observed in the young with subsequent autopsies indicating similar brain pathology in both age groups. Concurrently, there was progress in terms of subdividing dementias into several categories including vascular dementias, Alzheimer's type dementias, and sub-cortical dementias. Yet the term dementia did not disappear and continued to be a part of most diagnostic systems (e.g. DSM-III, DSM-IIIR, DSM-IV, ICD9, ICD10). Presumably, this reflects our general inability to precisely differentiate the various subtypes of dementia. Today, the term *dementia* remains a part of diagnostics despite advances in identifying disease-process specific subtypes.

THE COGNITIZATION OF DEMENTIA: DIAGNOSTIC ISSUES

Until the mid-1980's diagnostic criteria for dementia were referenced to the global disruption of function that were central to its presentation. Since 1984, however, dementia has been largely defined as a disorder of cognition. The turning point seems to have occurred with the publication of the NINCDS-ADRDA criteria, an event that marked the first sophisticated, systematized approach to the diagnosis of dementia (McKhann et al. 1984). The diagnostic systems used since then have been very specific about the need to focus on cognition. DSM-IV, for instance, focuses on the impairment or loss of specific cognitive abilities including memory, reasoning, praxis, language, and executive functioning and only peripherally on non-cognitive aspects of function. It is also interesting to note that the emphasis on cognition in post 1984 systems is almost exclusively on the need to document specific losses in specific areas. The idea of a more general or global loss of control that was central to historical views, and which still characterises the general medical view, largely disappeared.

COGNITION AND THE BRAIN

The cognitive centered view of dementia assumes a top-down organization of the brain in which the cognitive domain organizes and controls other aspects of human function. Even the strongest proponents of the cognitive perspective acknowledge that there are many non-cognitive phenomena which occur in the course of dementia. These features, however, are seen as either being derivative from the cognitive changes (which are in turn derivative from specific organic changes) or as being epiphenomenal. This assumption has, for good reason, been abandoned by modern cognitive science. In addition to having an outdated Cartesian flavour, the top-down view does not reflect current thinking about brain organization and function (Kandel, 1991).

Our knowledge of the actual working of the brain is somewhat limited. We do, however, know a few things. First, specific cognitive abilities are not stored in specific areas of the brain. Although there are areas of the brain that have specialized functions for language, visual processing, memory, etc., the phenomenon of memory, reasoning praxis, attention and others involve many different structural and functional processes. We also know that a disturbance in a cognitive output, such as speech, can be produced by a variety of structural and functional problems. Furthermore, it is reasonably well established that global disturbances of brain function tend to have a generally disruptive effect on all aspects of pre-cognitive, cognitive and behavioural function. This type of disruption is clearly seen in delirium/intoxication where there is disruption of function, as well as in hypoxia, and cases of accumulative insult where there is structural damage (Tune and Ross, 1994).

We also know that behaviour, temperament, emotionality, and many other functions are best understood as having an existence independent of cognition. IQ, our best current measure of overall cognitive ability for example, is not necessarily linked to temperament, behavioral sophistication, moral behavior, economic success, career choice or personality. Nor does it seem to have much to do with creativity, motor skills, or vocational preference. Cognitive abilities appear to be strongly correlated with cognitive tasks and weakly, if at all, with other aspects of behaviour. Research has also established that non-cognitive aspects of function, particularly temperament patterns, exist from birth and that adult personality reflects these in-born patterns of responsiveness. This is, no doubt, one of the main reasons that personality change occurs in the presence of acquired brain injury as well as one of the reasons why persons with mental handicap differ in personality and temperament.

Even in the presence of identifiable brain pathology, there is no strong and deterministic relationship between cognition and behavior. Individuals at the same level of mental handicap often present with entirely different patterns of behavioral strengths and weaknesses. Similarly, individuals with acquired brain injury who present with similar cognitive losses often exhibit grossly different behavioral and personality changes. What we have learned from work with those two populations is that a proper diagnosis and prognosis can be established only when there is full and proper assessment of function. No established diagnostic system, for example, permits the establishment of a diagnosis of mental handicap on the sole basis of cognitive impairment. There are precise requirements to establish the presence of both functional deficits and lack of adaptive capabilities. Particularly at the mild ranges of mental handicap, the cognitive impairment is seldom the determining factor in establishing the diagnosis. Nor is it acceptable practice to allow the determination of a diagnosis of acquired brain injury to rest solely on a cognitive evaluation. As is the case with mental handicap, the diagnostic evaluation must focus on a much wider array of both cognitive and non-cognitive variables. It is also known that damage in specific areas, such as the frontal lobe, produce marked behavioural changes in the absence of profound cognitive changes, although minor disturbances of cognition are often noted in such cases. The establishment of the diagnosis, then, includes both identifying causes of damage and accurately describing both the cognitive and non-cognitive sequlae (American Psychiatric Association, 1994).

The situation with dementia is interesting. Decades of research have demonstrated a number of cognitive deficits associated with the various types of dementia. At present, however, there is no convincing evidence of localized changes in structure to explain these deficits. The results of cognitive assessments in the early stages of dementia indicate: a) minor loss of expressive language skills without a localized neuroanatomical correlate, b) minor loss of memory function with, perhaps, a weak neuroanatomical correlate, c)loss of reasoning without a precise neuroanatomical correlate, d)Loss of praxic skill without a neuroanatomical correlate, e) loss of executive skills without a precise neuroanatomical correlate. This pattern, and indeed the specific observable deficits, is very different from those observed in the presence of discrete, localized lesions. Our interpretation is that the deficits are related in that each represents a cognitive failure that results from a diminished ability to control or regulate cortically moderated cognitive operations.

It is our contention, that cognitive changes are best understood not by tallying up the amount of dysfunction observed in multiple areas, but by analyzing the nature of the deficits that are observed. In fact, if we look at the precise patterns of dysfunction in each area an interesting picture emerges. The characteristic loss of memory is largely limited to recall of new information and a decreased ability to carry forward intentions to act. The language loss is largely limited to word-finding and fluency of output problems, both of which require intensive semantic processing and mental flexibility. Other aspects of language remain largely intact. The disturbance of praxis is initially limited to ideomotor tasks that involve the interpretation and application of spatial relationships (drawing complex figures, constructing shapes, etc.). The reasoning difficulties are very pronounced on tasks involving abstract problem solving and are much less apparent on tasks of similar difficulty involving concrete or socially based reasoning. Attention and concentration deficits occur not on simple attention measures such as vigilance tasks but are readily apparent on tasks involving complex processing such as counting backwards or in serial sequences. These deficits are not only fundamentally different from those found when there is specific regional damage, but appear to share the feature of being the result of involving complex, higher order information processing. To use a computer analogy, they seem to be software rather than hardware problems – a software problem that involves the operating system and which negatively effects the operation of all other complex software packages.

If, in fact, the cognitive problems observed in dementia initially stem from a loss of "systems control" then the same types of dyscontrol should be observed in other domains. The alternative, that there are functionally independent control systems for cognition and behaviour, is not easily supported by data on normal brain function, observations of individuals with acquired brain injuries, or persons with acute cortical dysfunction. Our analysis, in fact, leads us to expect that similar dyscontrol phenomena should be observed: a) on measures of cerebral function. b) in incidents of depressive and psychotic symptoms, and c) on measures of functional/behavioural change. The next section of this chapter looks at each of these areas and provides examples of changes that occur in the context of emerging dementias.

MARKERS OF A DEVELOPING DEMENTIA

DIGITAL EEG

There is reason to expect that the electrophysiology of the brain should show early impairment in dementias in general and in Alzheimer's disease in particular. To date, common wisdom is that EEG is not useful in early stages, but in later stages shows characteristic changes including temporal slow waves and epileptiform activity. Common wisdom may be wrong. At a conceptual level, any disease process significant enough to produce impairment of basic cognitive functions - globally - should produce some change in the electrophysiological function of either the cortex or the subcortical structures associated with cognition. At an empirical level, such changes have not been observed. Why?

The reason that EEG changes have not been observed in early dementias may be because traditional EEG, with paper tracings, generally measure brain waves up to approximately 30-35 Hz. This is not because EEG machines were designed to capture the full spectrum of electrical activity produced by the brain, but because the amplifiers and paper recorders were not capable of capturing activity much above those levels. As amplifier technology has improved, and as digital recording procedures have become available, it has become possible to measure higher frequency data. Such data as are presently available suggest that high frequency EEG activity occurs when the cortex is activated. In animal experiments, for example, researchers have documented bursts of 180-220 Hz activity that occurred during discrimination learning tasks. This is thought to reflect the cortical neuronal activity that occurs when an organism is learning a new task (Gaetz and Ancill, 1994).

Since new learning deficits are deemed to be a primary symptom of dementias, it is certainly interesting to ask what one might find if high frequency activity were measured in humans. We have started to answer that question. Using a high frequency digital EEG machine that measures activity in the range of 5 to 240 Hz. we have found that normal controls maintain a high level of EEG coherence at homologous frontal lobe sites. We have also gathered data indicating that the activity of persons with a clinical diagnosis of mild Alzheimer's disease exhibit a marked loss of EEG coherence.

Specifically, two patterns of diminished coherence were observed. The first pattern is characterized by a sudden lack of site coherence that occurs at approximately 80Hz and is, in contrast with normal age-matched controls, never re-established. The second pattern is characterized by a diminution of the normal range of coherence leading to a kind of hyper-coherence at the homologous frontal sites. We have also observed in several cases is that the second pattern, hyper-coherence at the frontal sites, is associated with a listless, apathetic, behaviorally flat presentation. These features were not observed in any patients showing the dramatic loss of coherence. The two groups, however, were indistinguishable in terms of their performance of classic cognitive measures including the MMSE, 3MS, and verbal learning tasks (Holliday, 1993).

Unfortunately, there is no high frequency EEG data available on persons in the very early stages of dementia. As such data become available, it will be possible to determine if high frequency changes are early signs of emerging dementia and, in particular, if cortical dysregulation is a central feature of dementia.

PSYCHIATRIC DISORDERS

Another interesting finding in the study of dementia is the occurrence of depression and psychosis in persons with dementia. Of particular importance is the completely unappreciated finding that depressive reactions may predate the occurrence of cognitive symptoms. The 1986 report by Agbayewa reported data demonstrating that emergent depression in elderly persons with no history of depressive illness was highly associated with the subsequent emergence of a dementia. It is now considered likely that single neurochemical models are not particularly compelling explanations of the emergence of psychiatric disorders, and it is quite possible that early changes in the acetylcholine system disrupt complicated balances of neurochemicals and can precipitate psychiatric symptoms. In short, neurochemical dysregulation may produce psychiatric disturbances that predate gross cognitive changes in the emergence of dementias.

The emergence of psychiatric problems in the course of dementias is also somewhat of a puzzle. If such psychiatric symptoms as paranoia and depression were simply a part of the global deterioration in the same manner as the cognitive symptoms, they would presumably appear in the majority of patients at a predictable time in the illness. This does not appear to be the case. They emerge at various times in an unpredictable fashion. It is also unappreciated that some types of psychotic symptoms in demented patients may respond to cholinomimetics.

Overall, it is not yet clear through what mechanism(s) psychiatric symptoms emerge in the course of dementias. It seems apparent, however, that the picture is neither simple nor uni-factorial. It is our opinion that a more thorough analysis of the emergence and treatment of psychiatric symptoms in the course of dementia are an important part of understanding the genesis and course of the dementing disorders.

FUNCTIONAL/BEHAVIOURAL CHANGES

When family members are closely questioned about the history of their loved one's illness, they often report that while memory loss was the first *florid* sign of an emerging dementia, there were subtle behaviour changes that predated the memory loss. The types of changes described include both the disappearance of complex patterns of behaviour and the emergence of inappropriate new behaviours (behaviour deficits and excesses). On the deficit side, some of the commonly reported occurrences include giving up recreational activities and hobbies, loosing interest in current events, becoming withdrawn, and just not being his/herself. It is not uncommon to find out, after close questioning, that family members had noticed, but not remarked on, such things as a person giving up knitting, loosing interest in long-established social activities, or becoming less skilled or dextrous at well-learned tasks. The emergence of negative behaviours can include inappropriate laughing, rude/unmannerly behaviour at the dinner table, inappropriate social encounters with strangers and so on.

Many family members will also report that the person with dementia exhibited subtle personality changes quite early in the course of the disorder. Not only do families report the occurrence of personality change; they tend to identify one of two patterns. In the first pattern, the person becomes less like their old self, while in the second, the person, in effect, becomes a characterized version of his/her premorbid self.

Both the functional and personality changes fall along the same dichotomized line as does the EEG data. The person either exhibits an exaggerated response or a diminished response. This suggests a diminishing of the regulatory process of the brain leaving the person either unable to inhibit responding or unable to initiate responding.

COGNITIZATION OF DEMENTIA: CLINICAL IMPLICATIONS

The movement to *cognitize* dementia is certainly in keeping with how North American medicine has a) misunderstood disorders of the brain and b) over-relied on standardized diagnostic procedures. We have a long history of conceptualizing brain disorders in terms of the most florid symptom. Thus we long insisted on defining schizophrenia in terms of hallucinations, and depression in terms of a gross mood change. Since the most florid symptoms of dementia (irrespective of the cause) are cognitive it is not surprising that they eventually came to be defined as the central features of dementia syndromes. What this approach encourages is the 'florid snapshot' diagnostic system whereby in chronic neuromedical illnesses the most obvious symptom or loss is seen as the defining element irrespective of where in the timecourse of the illness it occurs. If there is a commitment to establishing standardized diagnostic criteria, cognition appears to be particularly attractive. There are many standardized tests and procedures for assessing specific cognitive abilities - IQ tests for reasoning, verbal and visual learning tasks for assessing memory, tests of attention, tests of praxis, for example. There is also a relatively new field - neuropsychology - which claims special expertise in exactly this area. In short, the commitment to cognition carries with it the promise of a workable diagnostic methodology to objectify and quantify symptoms of dementia. This is similar to the rapid expansion of interest in the biogenic amine hypothesis of psychiatric illnesses in the 1960s and 1970s due in large part to the ability to measure the breakdown products of serotonin, norpepinephrine and dopamine in urine. Thus ease of measurement can make up for the shortfall in robust theory.

Unfortunately, this approach is both shortsighted and self-limiting. We know from our experience with schizophrenia, that the over-emphasis on florid symptoms can lead to initial gains but can also quickly lead the field down a blind alley. The uncritical acceptance of hallucinations and delusions as the core of schizophrenia which occurred during the 1960s and 1970s effectively blinded clinicians to the social impairment, mood disturbance, cognitive impairment and behavioural dysfunction that have historically been recognized as a part of the disorder. It has taken decades to have these features of the disease re-introduced to clinical diagnostics and practice. During their hiatus, we went through two decades of intensive development of therapeutic agents designed to control these symptoms. All of this work was motivated by the finding that dopamine was implicated in the occurrence of florid symptoms. Only after developing increasing potent dopamine blockers, did we discover that people whose hallucinations and delusions were controlled by these drugs did not actually get better. Presently, research is focusing on the development of broad-spectrum drugs as they appear to have a greater potential for actually treating the full spectrum of symptoms. In short, an inappropriate fixation on one aspect of a complex disease led to an abandonment of an older, and one which would ultimately prove to be richer, vision of schizophrenia.

We see the over-emphasis on cognition dementia, as creating a situation that is fundamentally similar to that which occurred with schizophrenia. It may be reasonable to accept cognition as the central focus of investigation if: a) it were shown to the best marker of dementia, b) it led to better diagnostics and management. and c) it led to the development of more effective therapeutics. As we have argued, there is considerable evidence arguing against a. We will now demonstrate, there is good reason to maintain that neither b nor c can be supported.

COGNITIZATION OF DEMENTIA: THERAPEUTIC IMPLICATIONS

As this chapter is being written, new treatment approaches for diseases characterised by progressive deterioration in brain function are being developed. The impetus for development derives mainly from the so-called "demographic imperative," that is, the relatively large number of citizens who are subject to increasing risk of dementia with their advancing age. Standard practices of institutional and environmental management for the dementing elderly are perceived as unpalatable by consumers, and are going to become increasingly costly for society to provide.

The search for better dementia treatments is fuelled by the recognition that currently available treatments are poor, or non-existent. Intervention, until very recently, has been entirely in the domains of palliation and treatment of derivative secondary symptoms, e.g., sleep disturbance. When the NINCDS-ADRDA narrowly defined dementia in 1984 as a disruption of cognition (and of memory in particular), the stage was set for industry and academic neuroscience to home in on compounds and treatments that would enhance cognition. This has led to the introduction of tacrine and donepezil to the American market, and to clinical trials of other agents.

As we have argued, dementias entail far more than just loss of intellectual prowess and mnemonic capacity. Destruction of brain tissue by vascular and neurodegenerative diseases that is the *sine qua non* of dementia also produces identifiable and problematic changes in personality, behaviour, mood, perception, and vegetative functions. Despite the emphasis on memory and cognition in the diagnosis of dementia and assessment of its response to intervention, the major watersheds of clinical decision-making have little or nothing to do with memory and cognition. For example, the decision to place an affected individual in institutional care generally hinges on functional parameters such as the presence of incontinence or wandering, rather than on the absolute degree of forgetfulness the person is manifesting.

If we learn from the experience with schizophrenia, we will eschew defining therapeutic efficacy for treatment of dementia as solely being improvement in memory or cognition. Instead, scientists and practitioners must review the assumptions and definitions of what constitutes a dementia, so that all the salient features of the illness can be targeted.

Presently, dementia treatments continue to be developed and tested in an intellectual environment that only acknowledges the cognitive features of dementia. The Consortium of Canadian Centres for Clinical Cognitive Research (C5R) enshrines the concept of cognition in the title of their organisation, yet purport to establish the fundamental theoretical basis on which all dementia treatments should be developed (Mohr et al., 1995). Just as highly successful treatments for schizophrenia would have been overlooked if our concept of the disease had remained solely that of positive symptoms and dopamine excess, the best treatment for patients with dementia seems unlikely to be discovered when therapeutic success is defined solely in terms of cognitive and mnemonic enhancement. And, in fact, neither the model of cognition (discrete abilities, top-down organization) that seems to underly dementia research nor the accepted methodology (standardized, global assessment scales such as the ADAS-COG) are, in our opinion, the most appropriate for studying the phenomenon of interest.

EVIDENCE-BASED THERAPEUTICS—WHAT EVIDENCE DO WE NEED?

The demand that medical interventions be "evidence-based" is our present zeitgeist. Rigorously controlled, double-blind, placebo-controlled studies are considered to be the gold standard for assessing efficacy of treatments. Decisions regarding the availability and funding of treatments are increasingly being tied to the existence of such research.

Presently, the evidence we have at hand regarding possible dementia treatments is only as good as the original hypotheses that were being addressed experimentally. As we have argued above, the theoretical framework within which anti-dementia drugs have been developed has been narrowly constructed around cognitive and memory deficits, and has not yet addressed any of the concurrent manifestations of dementia, such as personality change, mood symptoms, disruption of diurnal rhythms, and behavioural disturbance. It is an as-yet-unanswered question whether the current generation of Alzheimer disease treatments being brought to market (tacrine, donepezil, and others) will have beneficial impact on these other functions. The observation that a gain of two or three points on MMSE score (as seen with compounds such as tacrine) may be a clinically "trivial" improvement points out the fundamental flaws of investigations to date, rather than inherent difficulty with the drugs. We cannot yet make truly "evidence-based" decisions, as there is a dearth of quality evidence.

In the patient population that dementia treatments will be targeting, multi-system disease is the rule, rather than the exception. The vast majority of patients treated with any marketed dementia treatment will be on multiple medications, with additional disease processes that will potentially impact on CNS function. It must be asked, then, to what extent is it meaningful to try and extrapolate data from double-blind placebo controlled trials in "clean" subjects without comorbid disease to this population? There is a strong argument to be made for careful study of individual cases and case series, in the population that will ultimately be targeted with the treatment.

The icon of the placebo controlled study is rapidly becoming unethical to propose to patients and their families. To expect someone to risk no active treatment of a progressive, fatal condition when effective intervention is available is indefensible. As compounds such as tacrine and donepezil have become established as the current standard for the treatment of Alzheimer's disease, potential treatments in development will most properly be compared against these standards, rather than placebo.

As treatments with novel mechanisms of action are developed, based on richer understanding of the pathophysiology of dementing illnesses, it will eventually be necessary to address the relative efficacy of combination treatment versus a single agent. There is certainly precedent for this kind of clinical and investigational approach in other domains of medicine, such as oncology and infectious diseases. There is good reason to believe that a person with Alzheimer's disease treated with a cholinesterase inhibitor, a cholinergic agonist, an anti-oxidant, an anti-inflammatory, and a neurotrophic will have more potential for improvement and delay of disease progression than a patient treated with any single modality alone. To ignore this possibility makes neither clinical nor academic sense.

REFERENCES

American Psychiatric Association (1994) Diagnostic and Statistical Manual of Mental Disorders, 4th edition. Washington, DC: American Psychiatric Association

Canadian Pharmaceutical Association (1997) Compendium of pharmaceuticals and specialities. *Canadian Pharmaceutical Association*: Ottawa, ON

Gaetz M, Ancill RJ (1994) Exploring the positive and negative symptom continuum using high-frequency digital EEG. In, *Schizophrenia: Exploring the Spectrum of Psychosis*, London: John Wiley & Sons

Holliday SG (1991) High Frequency Digital EEG, *unpublished report*, St. Vincent's Hospital

Kandel E (1991) Brain and behaviour. In, Principles of Neural Sciences (eds Kandel E, Schwartz, J and Jessel T), 3rd edition, London: Appleton and Large

Krapelin E (1909) Dementia praecox and paraphrenia. In *Kraepelin's Textbook of Psychiatry*, 8th edition, Barclay R (trans.) Edinburgh: Livingston,1919.

McKhann G, Drachmav D, Folstein ME, et al., (1984) Clinical diagnosis of Alzheimer's disease: report of the NINCDS-ADRDA group under the auspices of the Department of Health and Human Services Task Force on Alzheimer's Disease. *Neurology:* 34: 939-944

Mohr E, Feldman H & Gauthier S (1995) Canadian guidelines for the gevelopment of antidementia therapies: a conceptual summary. *Canadian Journal of Neurological Science* 22: 62-71

Tune L and Ross C (1994) Delirium, In *Textbook of Geriatric neuropsychology* (eds Coffey C and Cummings J), Washington, DC: American Psychiatric Press Inc.

Index

Note: page numbers in *italics* refer to figures and tables

dementia, vascular (*cont.*)
  neuropathology 16
  oxygen free radicals in pathogenic
      cascade 24
  risk factors 18–19
  secondary prevention 20–2
  symptomatic/stabilization therapy
      22–3
  treatment strategies 18–20
demyelination, ischemic in white matter
    of brain 82–3
deprenyl 4
depression 37–8
  adrenal function 97
  antiglucocorticoids 105, 106
  caregiver stress 37
  causes 39
  chronic pain 74, 75
  co-morbid with dementia 121–2
  cognitive–behavioural therapies
      138–9
  cortisol antagonist therapy 105–6
  cortisol levels 103
  cortisol and stressful life events 97
  Cushing's disease 96–7
  dementia 41, 146–7
  differential diagnosis 39–41
    from delirium 65–6
  diseases presenting as 40
  drug-induced 40
  electroconvulsive therapy 48–9, 79,
      80
  hypercortisolism 98
  incidence 37
  melancholic 87
  neurovegetative symptoms 38–9
  Parkinson's disease 5–6
  pharmacological management 41–2
  post-stroke 82
  presentation 38–9
  psychotherapy 138–9
  rate of onset 66
  recognition *38*
  recurrent 66
  strategies for achieving maximum
      antidepressant efficacy 47–8
  treatment 38
    in dementia 80
    options 42
desipramine 46

dexamethasone 99, 100
  cortisol effects 105
  sensitivity/resistance 97
diabetes mellitus 18
disorder-event disorder cycle 97
disorientation 123, 124
domperidone 2
donezepil 150, 151
doxepin 6, 46
drugs
  augmentation 48
  combination 47
  compliance 41–2
  depressogenic 40
  half-life in elderly 41
  metabolic clearance 85
  optimization 47
  strategies for achieving maximum
      antidepressant efficacy 47–8
  substitution 47–8
  see also medication
dysergastic reaction 61
dyskinesia 4
  levodopa treatment 3

electroconvulsive therapy (ECT)
    79–89
  administration to patient with
      dementia 85–7
  anticonvulsants 89
  bilateral 87
  cardiovascular effects 87
  cognitive impairment 84–5
  complications 87
  contraindications 85
  delirium 84–5
  dementia 49, 80–3
  depression 48–9
  duration of treatment 85–6
  frequency 85–6
  general anaesthesia 88
  memory impairment 84
  Parkinson's disease 6, 8
  premedication 87
  seizure threshold 88
  stimulus
    administration 86–7
    parameters 86
  treatment
    interactions 88–9

Index compiled by Jill Halliday